No More "Look Up the List" Vocabulary Instruction

Dear Readers,

Much like the diet phenomenon *Eat This, Not That*, this series aims to replace some existing practices with approaches that are more effective—healthier, if you will—for our students. We hope to draw attention to practices that have little support in research or professional wisdom and offer alternatives that have greater support. Each text is collaboratively written by authors representing research and practice. Section 1 offers a practitioner's perspective on a practice in need of replacing and helps us understand the challenges, temptations, and misunderstandings that have led us to this ineffective approach. Section 2 provides a researcher's perspective on the lack of research to support the ineffective practice(s) and reviews research supporting better approaches. In Section 3, the author representing a practitioner's perspective gives detailed descriptions of how to implement these better practices. By the end of each book, you will understand both what not to do, and what to do, to improve student learning.

It takes courage to question one's own practice—to shift away from what you may have seen throughout your years in education and toward something new that you may have seen few if any colleagues use. We applaud you for demonstrating that courage and wish you the very best in your journey from this to that.

Best wishes,
— *Nell K. Duke and Ellin Oliver Keene, series editors*

No More "Look Up the List" Vocabulary Instruction

CHARLENE COBB

CAMILLE BLACHOWICZ

HEINEMANN
Portsmouth, NH

Heinemann
361 Hanover Street
Portsmouth, NH 03801–3912
www.heinemann.com

Offices and agents throughout the world

The authors and publisher wish to thank those who have generously given permission to reprint borrowed material:

Excerpts from Common Core State Standards © Copyright 2010. National Governors Association Center for Best Practices and Council of Chief State School Officers. All rights reserved.

Library of Congress Cataloging-in-Publication Data
Cobb, Charlene.
   No more "look up the list" vocabulary instruction / Charlene Cobb and Camille Blachowicz.
      pages cm. – (Not this, but that)
   Includes bibliographical references.
   ISBN 978-0-325-04920-5
   1. Vocabulary—Study and teaching.   I. Blachowicz, Camille L. Z.
II. Title.

LB1574.5.C63 2014
372.44—dc23   2013037893

Series editors: Nell K. Duke and Ellin Oliver Keene
Editor: Margaret LaRaia
Production: Vicki Kasabian
Interior design: Suzanne Heiser
Cover design: Lisa A. Fowler
Cover photo: Jamie Grill / The Image Bank / Getty Images
Typesetter: Valerie Levy, Drawing Board Studios
Manufacturing: Veronica Bennett

Printed in the United States of America on acid-free paper
18   17   16   15   14   VP   1   2   3   4   5

To my wonderful students,
past, present, and future
—Camille

To my husband Peter, our wonderful children,
and our amazing grandchildren
—Charlene

CONTENTS

SECTION 3   **BUT THAT**

42   **Flexible Instruction for Vocabulary Learning**

Camille Blachowicz and Charlene Cobb

ACKNOWLEDGMENTS

We would like to acknowledge all the educators who have so generously allowed us in their classrooms and schools. Thanks to the teachers, literacy specialists, academic achievement coaches, and administrators of East Maine District 63. A special note of thanks to the teachers, reading specialists, and administrators of Evanston-Skokie District 65, especially those at Washington School, and to the members of the Reading Leadership Institute.

INTRODUCTION

ELLIN OLIVER KEENE

When Nell and I discussed the concept for Not This, But That, vocabulary instruction, specifically look-it-up-and-define-it practices, were among the first topics we thought about for the series. We talked about how ingrained these practices are and how often they're part of daily fare in classrooms and that parents actually *demand* that their children be given long vocabulary lists to look up and define. I was the mom demanding that students *not* be asked to do it.

At the time, my daughter had just been accepted to college and I told Nell, the mother of very young children, about the horror of tearful nights at our house when Elizabeth left the vocabulary list lookup until all the other homework was complete and cried (at 11:30 P.M.) as she faced the boredom of looking up twenty to thirty words and creating sentences in which the context revealed her understanding of the word. The final straw came late one night when she defined *verisimilitude* and wrote the following sentence: "We should avoid verisimilitude." I was so exasperated, knowing that she was unlikely to remember the words she was defining that I actually said, "Just go with it, honey. You're already into college."

She knew it wasn't working to build her vocabulary, I knew it wasn't working, as did hundreds of my colleagues who continued the practice because alternatives were not well understood. This book changes that forever and I hope it saves hundreds of students and their parents from late-night meltdowns!

For that, we have to thank Dr. Charlene Cobb and Dr. Camille Blachowicz, coauthors of this book. Char is Assistant Superintendent of Teaching and Learning in East Maine School District 63 in Des Plaines, Illinois. She brings experience as a teacher, reading specialist, and assistant superintendent to the immediately useful vocabulary practices in this book. Camille is Professor Emeritus and Co-Director of the Reading Leadership Institute at National–Louis University in Chicago. Camille has a long-standing record in undertaking research on vocabulary and then expertly translating it into useful classroom practices.

In Section 2, Camille reminds us that understanding word meaning is one of the most significant factors that influence reading comprehension. We believe that it is critical that teachers discontinue ineffective practices and immerse students in learning situations that will lead to incidental and intentional vocabulary learning of the "Flood, Fast, Focus" variety Char and Camille suggest. Of all the useful practices they describe, one through-line that stood out to me: *Engagement in word learning is key.* Kids should have choice in at least some of the words they learn, and they need teachers who discuss and model their own excitement about words. When adults show how fascinated they are by words and how much fun it can be to engage in wordplay and grow our word knowledge, children will follow suit. Char and Camille both make the case for new and engaging practices and provide teachers with dozens of them that can be applied in classrooms tomorrow.

In a study Camille cites in Section 2, a student actually uttered the following words, "I used to only think about vocabulary in school. The whole world is vocabulary." Wouldn't that be music to your ears coming from one of your students? We believe that this book will help you make that viewpoint common among your students. We encourage you to experiment with the ideas in this book and to familiarize yourself with the research Camille synthesizes so clearly so that you can help others, including parents, understand that vocabulary learning is (mercifully) different than they remember. When you're done with this book, pass it on to colleagues. There are far too many children in this country writing sentences like "We should avoid verisimilitude" at 11:30 at night. And, really, once you know what *verisimilitude* means, it's a very useful word and it sounds cool to say too! Happy word learning!

NOT THIS

"Look 'Em Up, Write the Definition, Write a Sentence"

CHARLENE COBB

In middle school, my youngest daughter's vocabulary instruction re-sided within the pages of a little book with a series of lessons. Each lesson focused on twenty words and a set of activities such as finding synonyms for the words, making analogies, or completing a crossword puzzle. To this day, my daughter remembers two words from the pro-gram, *saboteur* and *espionage*. Now, my daughter is neither a spy nor an author of action thrillers, but she held onto those words because she liked to say them. That kind of authentic pleasure in the sounds of language is something to be celebrated, but it wasn't taught to her. It was a happy circumstance. The planned "instruction"—playing a few games in a workbook—wasn't enough, and the majority of those words in that little vocabulary workbook stayed right where they were.

Learning Words Means Using Them

For many of us, the vocabulary instruction we received (or in some cases endured) consisted primarily of looking up a list of words, writing the definition, and/or writing a sentence with the word, then a quiz on the definitions. This weekly process repeated itself, like the cycle of a washing machine, each time emptied of what came before. We couldn't hold onto our word knowledge because our grasp was limited by the brief weeklong encounter with the words. There was little expectation of repeated encounters with these words and even less expectation of using the words in our reading and writing. As you'll learn in Section 2, there are different levels of understanding a word's meaning, but without practice in the full range of ways we use a word, our word knowledge is limited and falls from our grasp as the next cycle of words enter.

We Need to Question the Way We Were Taught

Most students don't enjoy learning words the "look-up-the-list" way (except that they're an easy A for some) and neither do teachers. Yet we continue to teach this way. Why? Like most of us, we default to teaching the way we were taught. I'll admit that I did. I might not have enjoyed teaching that way, but I didn't consider doing it differently until I was shown another way. As I learned more, I began to evaluate my current practice rather than passively replicating how I had been taught. I know that teachers work hard and often hold themselves to the unrealistic expectation of reinventing everything. This book is not about discarding everything you are already doing. I believe that we do the best we can with the knowledge we have, but then when we know more, we do better. Instead of just working harder, perhaps teachers could work smarter by finding out what the latest research says about best practice and asking ourselves if there's a better way to provide vocabulary instruction.

Why We Struggle with Change

I began working as a reading specialist nearly twenty-five years ago. Over those twenty-five years, I have been a reading specialist, district-level administrator, and university instructor, and I have been lucky to work with many amazing teachers. Unfortunately, vocabulary instruction has remained almost the same as it was when I started my career in education. I still see vocabulary workbooks, but in some cases vocabulary workbooks have been replaced with work sheets or computer programs. Materials may look different, but students are still presented with fifteen to twenty words per week. Content-area vocabulary too often focuses on boldface words and the use of glossaries as the main source of word definition. Why is that? With all that is known about best practices for teaching and learning vocabulary, as you'll see in Section 2, why are we still teaching vocabulary in the least effective ways?

Teachers' Common Questions, Familiar Answers, and Some Considerations for Change

We start with the fundamental question: How can we teach vocabulary so that students can become better readers and writers? Within this, in conversations with teachers about vocabulary instruction, I hear the same four concerns (see Figure 1–1):

How does research answer these questions?

see Section 2, page 20

- How many words should I teach and how do I select them?
- How can I foster student independence using resources such as dictionaries and glossaries?
- How can I find time for meaningful vocabulary instruction when I need to focus on so many other priorities in the curriculum?
- How can I assess and hold students accountable, especially when some students don't remember the words that I teach?

Figure 1–1

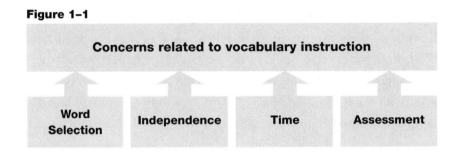

These are all legitimate issues, raised by teachers who are committed to their students' growth. The purpose of this section is to think about which practices we want to change and why, so let's take a look at each concern and evaluate how teachers commonly address it in their classrooms.

Word Selection: How do I select words and when should I teach them?

I'm never sure if I'm choosing too many words or too few. When I'm teaching with a novel, I usually select a few words from each section or chapter. You know, the ones that I'm pretty sure the students won't understand. If they don't know the word, then they won't comprehend what they're reading. If I select three to five words in a book with ten chapters, they end up with thirty to fifty words for each novel. Sometimes I can find words that have already been selected from lesson plans online or words that other people have already used. I have the students do their vocabulary as independent work. They look the words up in the dictionary and write a sentence using the word.

Many new teachers, and even experienced teachers, lack confidence in their ability to select vocabulary words from novels. They want students to be able to read and understand the text, but they recognize that some words will be too difficult. This can occur more frequently when an entire class is reading the same novel. With only one text, some students are sure to struggle and others will have little to no difficulty with new words. For teachers who use multiple novels, selecting words from three or more texts can be a daunting endeavor. Whether selecting from one novel or multiple novels, students are expected to define and learn an extensive list of words. This may be why teachers frequently relay on external sources such as novel units, or lessons posted on Internet sites. However, whether teachers select the words themselves or use other resources, frequently the sheer volume of words means that the task may become disconnected from the primary goal of reading and comprehending the book. More importantly, looking up a word that is isolated from the text often does not enable students to understand that word when they encounter it in context.

> Our science and social studies textbooks have all the important words for each section presented on the first page. They give the student the word and sometimes also a brief definition. We always go over those words before we start reading. Sometimes I assign vocabulary for homework. I have the students look up the words in the glossary and then use them in a sentence. There's always at least one work sheet that has some kind of vocabulary activity. Sometimes we do them together as a class, or the students work on it independently.

Many teachers rely on the textbook publishers' word selection. And in fact, many of the words selected by publishers are important words. But understanding content-area texts involves more than learning the meaning of the boldface words. Learning content vocabulary is reliant on students' prior knowledge and their level of understanding of the concepts represented by the vocabulary. This can be especially problematic for second language learners who may not have

For examples of content-area vocabulary practices

see Section 3, pages 52–65

the background knowledge needed for deep understanding of the concepts presented. Additionally, the internal structures of content-area texts can make them more difficult to read. In addition to the words related to the content topic, students need to understand the process and function words that repeatedly occur in science and social studies texts. For example, process words and phrases such as *state a conclusion, draw a summary,* and *skim/scan the text* or function words such as *therefore, moreover,* and *in conclusion,* can be challenging for many students, but especially second language learners.

In both of these scenarios, teachers are relying on external sources in determining the words selected for instruction. There is a certain comfort level for teachers in using an outside, authoritative source. But not all word lists and definitions are of equal value. The teacher is an essential mediator. The individual teacher needs to evaluate which words are most needed by her students and to identify meaningful opportunities for students to use and develop their understanding of the words. If we only pass on a decontextualized list to our students, we reinforce the idea that words are not owned but borrowed from someone else. In Sections 2 and 3, we will share some ways to think about how to select words, how many words to teach, and some engaging ways to teach them.

Independence: How can I help my students become independent word learners?

For ideas on developing independent word learners

see Section 3, pages 44–45

When we are doing a novel unit, I usually give the students a list of words for the upcoming sections we'll be reading. One of the things I have them do is look the words up in the dictionary before we read. This helps with vocabulary, and also gives them practice as independent word learners. Even in the intermediate grades, some of the students come without any dictionary skills. They don't know how to use the guide words at the top of the page, and they have no idea what the pronunciation guide means. So I'm able to kill two birds with one stone. They are learning the meaning of the words they'll see in the novel and they are also learning how to use resources for looking up words. I will either teach or review some of the dictionary skills when I introduce the words. Then I give them time to practice their dictionary skills with the words from the novel.

With science and social studies, I have students use the glossaries. I want them to know that they should look for these tools when they are reading. Our new science book has definitions placed in the margins, but I still want them to understand how important it is to use the glossary.

It's true that it is important for students to know how to use a variety of resources related to vocabulary. It's also true that students need to understand the external features of texts, such as glossaries. Many teachers I've worked with realize that instruction related to these is not highly effective if done in isolation, so I rarely see work sheets on using guide words. In most of the schools in which I work, teachers realize the value of these skills and so they incorporate them into novel studies and content instruction. The problem with most definitional approaches to vocabulary instruction is that they generally lead to more superficial understanding: Looking up words in the dictionary does not necessarily improve comprehension. Dictionary definitions are most helpful if you already have some understanding of the concept or word meaning. Many definitions don't contain enough information to enable you to use the word accurately. The word *run* provides a perfect example of this dilemma. There are more than one hundred definitions of the word *run* in *Webster's New Collegiate Dictionary* (1979). These definitions cover nearly the entire page in the dictionary. The word is defined as a verb, a noun, and an adjective. Now imagine a second language student reading the following sentences in a social studies text. "In 1858 Abraham Lincoln challenged Stephen Douglas for his seat in the U.S. Senate. He lost that election. But the debates he held with Douglas led to his run for the presidency in 1860." In these sentences, the word *run* is the thirteenth definition: "to enter into an election contest." Most students go for the first definition, which in this case is "to go faster than a walk" (1005). Now let's make it a bit more confusing by asking the student to define *seat*. The correct definition is found in the first line, "a special chair of one in eminence: the status represented." Yes, easy to find, but not so easy to understand.

I vividly remember a fifth-grade student who was reading a book about a group of boys out for a walk on a dark night. They were hoping to convince another group of boys to join them. The words of the text went something like, "It was already dark. John was nervous. He didn't think they had a ghost of a chance." When I asked the student to tell me about the story, he explained, "The boy was nervous about seeing a ghost." He had mapped the words *dark night, nervous boy,* and *ghost* to create an incorrect summary. Looking up the word *ghost* would be of no help to this student. What he needed was an understanding of the figure of speech.

Content-area words with multiple meanings abound and confuse students. Consider these words: *yard, current, sink, bear, plane,* and *pound.* How would you define *current* in social studies and in science? How about *plane* in math and in social studies? We need to be thoughtful and intentional as we select the words we teach our students and what we ask students to do with these words. Nevertheless, this process of giving students a list and asking them to look up the words persists in many classrooms. The simplicity of looking words up in a dictionary or glossary supersedes our discomfort in doing something that we sense is not highly effective. Our belief in the need for repeated practice of skills supplants our thinking that this practice is not necessarily improving our primary goal of greater comprehension.

And in some cases, we just don't know what else to do, so we rely on doing things the same way we were taught.

I don't want to give the impression dictionaries or glossaries should not be used as word-learning resources. While traveling recently, I used a GPS (global positioning system) to find a route to a specific location. As I struggled to find my way (even with the help of the GPS as a resource), I came to see the analogy of a dictionary to a GPS system. Let me explain. This was the first time I had ever traveled to this area. I knew nothing about the location I was trying to find. I had an address. I entered the address and a set of directions appeared. I had some options such as fastest route and least use of tollways. I set my course and began driving. Oh, by the way, I was alone in the car. As I struggled to listen to the directions, pay attention to the road signs, and make the right decisions, I discovered that a road was closed. The GPS didn't know this and so it kept trying to return me to a route that was impossible. I eventually found my way, but not without a significant amount of work on my part. So how is a GPS like a dictionary? They are both resources that guide us to a destination (location or word meaning). They both are more effective if you know a little bit about where you are going when you start the journey. They can both take you to an incorrect place, and it's always helpful to have someone else along for the journey (see Figure 1–2).

I will not stop using a GPS system, just as I would not encourage teachers and students to stop using dictionaries and other resources. Rather, I encourage teachers to think more broadly about their use. Do students understand what it means to "know" a word and how this knowledge develops over time? How can students work collaboratively to generate word meanings? Are students able to transfer their word learning from a dictionary definition to other texts? What other experiences might they need to help them do so? Do the words they

For a better framework for vocabulary instruction

see Section 2, page 28

Figure 1–2 Why Using a Dictionary Is Like Using Your GPS

Resource	Dictionary	GPS	Analogy
Goal	You are trying to get the specific meaning of a word.	You are trying to get to a specific location.	I need specific information.
The resource as a support	You know a little bit about the word and you are seeking greater clarification.	You have knowledge of your location and you are seeking validation or the best route.	OK—this makes sense, I can do this.
Overreliance on the resource	You have no idea what the word means and you end up with an incorrect definition.	You are in unfamiliar surroundings and end up lost.	I have no idea where this is taking me.
Guidance	You share your thinking with a peer or teacher to ensure accuracy.	You have a passenger who can adjust the settings or choose an alternate route.	It's so much easier when I have support!

look up enable them to become better readers and writers? For students to become independent word learners, we need to do more than refer them to a resource. We need to give them a collection of strategies and resources to support them as they navigate their own word learning.

And, we need to be mindful of the obstacles we may be putting in their way. When a teacher stops a read-aloud too often to verbally define words she thinks kids don't know, it's the equivalent of tossing too many balls to a juggler: The kids become distracted from comprehending the text and won't retain the words introduced either. In content-area instruction, students are often asked to play the vocabulary guessing game: "Does anyone know what xxx means? OK, yeah, kind of, anyone else, OK, yeah, that's close. . . ." These practices communicate an expectation that students should know and hold onto the words without giving them the resources and support to do so. Students who don't know or can't retain the words often interpret their lack of success as a deficit in their capacity. That's the opposite of independence. In the next two sections, you'll learn ways to help students realize that words are something they can acquire and that by learning the right strategies, they can be successful, independent word learners.

Time: How can I find time for vocabulary instruction?

Oh, there's never enough time, that's why I have students do most of their vocabulary work during their independent time or I give it as homework. We have ninety minutes a day for both reading and writing. If I'm trying to do readers' and writers' workshop, I need at least thirty minutes for my small-group reading and another thirty minutes for small-group writing. I try to do some modeling and that means another ten to fifteen minutes in both reading and writing. I'm also supposed to find time for them to do independent reading and to confer with the students on those books! I'm lucky if I get some vocabulary instruction in once a week.

I probably spend a little more time on vocabulary for science and social studies because they have to know those words. It's also easier to point out the words that the students need to know because they are usually boldface or highlighted in some way. Also, many times there are vocabulary worksheets or activities already available in the teacher resources. But I usually assign them for homework. Content-area words that express abstract concepts are particularly hard. How do you teach the word *economy* or *relativity*? We do spend a lot of time talking about the content and so there are opportunities to talk about some of the words. But sometimes students don't seem to remember the words if they come up just a few weeks later in another unit.

In the middle school, we have so much content to cover and so little time. I only see my students for forty-three minutes a day. In that time, I have to teach them about the content and give them time to talk and write about it as well. The content words they need to know are highlighted in the textbook. I do encourage them to use the glossary at the back of the book. Also, with the online version of our text that some students use at home, they can click on any of the highlighted words and have the word and the definition read to them. Sometimes for homework I'll have students explain the important words from the chapter in their own words. Many of the students just reword the definition from the text into a sentence, so I'm not sure how much they're really learning about the word. I have a degree in social studies, and I didn't take any reading methods courses. I've learned about teaching content vocabulary at some workshops and the district has provided some professional development on content-area reading, but I'm not very comfortable taking time away from teaching the content to do those types of vocabulary activities.

Teachers and students are always prisoners of time. Teachers are always being asked to do more, but the length of the school day remains the same. In intermediate and junior high classrooms, the emphasis is generally on reading comprehension and writing composition. Teachers are expected to "cover" the anthology or novels within specified time frames. When teachers use only one text, they feel the need to spend additional time supporting comprehension instruction for students who find the text too difficult. Vocabulary is frequently marginalized to independent work or homework.

In most junior high and middle schools, social studies and science are taught departmentally. Social studies and science teachers enjoy teaching their content. They've worked hard to become experts. Many have not had opportunities to learn the most effective methods of incorporating vocabulary instruction into their lessons. Add to this the fact that many of the content texts are difficult for students reading below level and extremely difficult for second language learners who lack the background knowledge needed to access the content. In both elementary and middle school classrooms, I see a significant amount of reading aloud by both students and teachers during science and social studies. Teachers spend time explaining the content, and there are some rich discussions occurring. These discussions are important. They support students' oral language development and provide opportunities to talk about words. However, discussions alone are not enough for students to develop a deep level of word meaning. Students need opportunities to read and practice using the words in meaningful ways.

Again, it's little wonder that in these classrooms vocabulary instruction can be minimal. Finding time for vocabulary instruction is directly related to the other three issues: Teachers need to be thoughtful in the words that they select for vocabulary instruction, they need to think broadly about moving beyond dictionaries and word lists as the primary source of word learning, and they must use instruction and assessment interactively. We can't always change the amount of time we are allotted, but we can change the structures and methods we use to deliver instruction.

Assessment: How can I assess and hold students accountable?

I have to have some way of evaluating vocabulary. I've used the vocabulary assessments that go along with the units from core reading programs, textbook chapter word lists, and online

For ideas of more effective assessment practices

see Section 3, pages 72, 74–80

word lists for novels to create multiple-choice tests. Sometimes I'll try to vary the format and have students match the word to the correct definition. I like to have several assessments each quarter so that I can average the scores to come up with the grade. For science and social studies, it's much easier because there are always one or two vocabulary questions on the unit tests.

It's frustrating that vocabulary tests are a lot like spelling tests. Many students get good scores on their test, but then don't ever use the word correctly again. Also, in science or social studies, it seems like they understand the word while we're learning it, but if it comes up again or in a context other than social studies, they don't make the connection.

This response reflects the realities and the frustrations many teachers feel when it comes to assessing vocabulary. It also brings forward the concern that as data from state and national assessments are analyzed, the vocabulary scores may point to the need for improvement. How do we measure that learning and improvement? Relying solely on outside resources (including textbooks) for vocabulary selection and assessment is not the right answer, but it's an easy one. However, when given the task of designing assessments, it's little wonder that teachers model their self-created tests on those commercial tests they've used in the past. Many teachers don't have access to a better model.

Teacher-created assessments can be another area of frustration. Constructing assessments can be time-consuming, and some teachers lack confidence in their ability to create valid tests. In middle school and junior high content classes, a vocabulary test provides one opportunity for students to demonstrate their word knowledge. Once the test is graded and the unit is completed, instruction moves on to the next topic. There is rarely time to go back and revisit the vocabulary from previous chapters.

This type of vocabulary assessment is based on the traditional input–outcome aspect of teaching and learning. Input: The teacher selects the content (vocabulary words) and delivers instruction to the students. Output: The teacher tests the students on the content. The scores from the content determine the grade. Notice that the input–outcome model is light on the aspect of *learning*. How many of us have heard (or even said), "I taught it, but they didn't learn it"? In Section 2 we will show how research has repeatedly informed us that word learning is incremental. Word learning is also dependent upon the students' prior knowledge. When we assess students, we have to consider that they may have memorized a definition that can be attached to a label, but they may not have developed the depth of conceptual and word knowledge needed to know this word and use it flexibly in other situations. An end of the unit, multiple-choice assessment does not yield this type of information. This leads us to question: How can we assess students in ways that measure the full understanding of words?

Of course it's difficult to change the method of assessment without also considering the methods of instruction. When I work with teachers, I encourage them to think about teaching and assessing as a continuum. I want teachers to realize that students need opportunities to increase both their breadth and depth of word knowledge. I want students to increase the number of words they have in their receptive and expressive vocabularies. But I also want them to know a word at multiple levels, across a variety of contexts. I want teachers to think about the importance of word-learning strategies. I also ask them to begin thinking differently about assessing vocabulary. Can word-learning strategies such as word sorts, knowledge ratings, and concept of definition frames be used as diagnostic, formative, and summative assessments? If we move away from the "list, define, create a sentence" structure of teaching, can that support a more informed assessment process? Perhaps it might be time to start thinking differently about teaching and assessing vocabulary.

To learn how instruction and assessment can support one another

see Section 3, pages 71–72

Effective Vocabulary Instruction in Every Classroom

Up to this point, we've shared some concerns teachers have regarding vocabulary instruction. But if we're honest, there are some classrooms where vocabulary instruction does not occur. As districts and schools transition to the Common Core State Standards, this is no longer an option. The Common Core State Standards recognize the importance of vocabulary instruction kindergarten through grade 12. In *Appendix A: Research Supporting the Key Elements of the Standards* (National Governors Association Center for Best Practices and Council of Chief State School Officers 2010b), the authors of Common Core state, "The importance of students acquiring a rich and varied vocabulary cannot be overstated" (32). Expectations for vocabulary are found in Reading Standard 4, for both Literature and Informational Texts, and also in the Language Standards 4–6. The level of rigor for vocabulary increases across grade levels.

In the intermediate grades, students are expected not only to understand figurative language, but also to analyze the impact of these words on the meaning of the text. Within the Language Standards, students are expected to acquire and use general academic and domain-specific vocabulary that is grade-level appropriate. The intent of the Common Core State Standards is for students to develop rich and flexible word knowledge.

In the next section, Camille will share the research related to best practices in vocabulary instruction. Then in Section 3 we will share some strategies and techniques that invite you to start thinking differently about vocabulary instruction in your classroom!

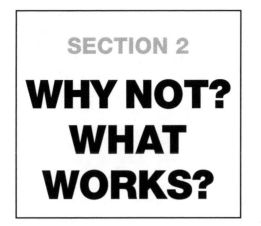

SECTION 2

WHY NOT? WHAT WORKS?

What We Know About Vocabulary Acquisition and What It Means for Instruction

CAMILLE BLACHOWICZ

What's Lost When We Tell Students to "Look Up the List"

Let's be honest. Most teachers (including me) have, at one time or another, put a list of words on the board and asked students to look them up. Maybe the practice was done in the heat of the moment: We were rushed for time or needed students to occupy themselves while we handled something more urgent (like someone throwing up in the back of the classroom). But if we reflect on what was happening in students' heads while they filled time (see Figure 2–1), we realize that this work neither developed students' deep understanding of words nor communicated how word knowledge can give students power. Further, "list lookup" does not have a strong foundation in research. Moreover, there is significant research on student difficulty in carrying out the process (McKeown 1993).

Figure 2–1

What's Happening in Students' Heads **While They're Looking Up the List?**
Hmm, the word is *GLIPPLE*. Let's see. . . . [finding it in the dictionary] OK, GLIPPLE . . . hmm let's look . . . I see *GLIPPLE*, OK . . . I know I should write the first definition but that will take me forever. Here's the shortest definition. I'll write that. OK, definition done.   Now a sentence. OK, it's a verb. How about, "I decided to *GLIPPLE*." No, she'll catch on if I do that and just have it the last word. How about "I *GLIPPLED* yesterday." Yeah, that's it. Done.

In Section 1, Char shared some of teachers' common struggles with vocabulary instruction: word selection, student independence in resource use, assessment, and the bugaboo, time. Before I was a teacher educator and researcher, I was a classroom teacher who struggled with these same issues. I became a teacher through what is now called the "alternative route to certification." As the newest, and most underprepared, teacher in an urban school, I was given the *C* group, students in third, fourth, and fifth grade who struggled in reading and writing. My clearest memory from my first six months of teaching was returning from school to lie on my bed and crying while my graduate-student husband patted the back of his working wife, worrying that we might be en route to unemployment and poverty.

Like so many teachers who must teach struggling students without being prepared for it, I worked hard to rise to the occasion because I fell in love with the kids. The struggling students in my classes were smart, many negotiating life challenges that most adults would find daunting, but their limited word knowledge, background knowledge, or other limiting factors made it difficult for them to develop their understanding of essential concepts and to build background knowledge. As I studied for my certification, I was buoyed by research that suggested I was on the right track (Bos and Anders 1990, 1992). Now, with the emphasis on vocabulary in current initiatives such as the Common Core State Standards (CCSS; National Governors Association Center for Best Practices and Council of Chief State School Officers 2010a), it's a great time to revisit and refresh our understandings of why vocabulary matters to all students, both the typical and the struggling.

Word knowledge matters. When students struggle with reading in their language arts and content-area classes, a very important part of their struggle is with vocabulary. Word knowledge is an essential tool to "do school" and to "do reading" that they are missing often because of different language or cultural backgrounds and limited exposure to the language used in school. And without vocabulary knowledge, comprehension suffers (Stahl and Fairbanks 1986). Knowledge of meaning vocabulary has long been recognized as one of the most important correlates to reading comprehension (Wagner, Muse, and Tannenbaum 2007; Davis 1944, 1968; Terman 1916). Yet because it is not only print-bound but also reflects experience with the world and with language (Hart and Risley 1995), it affects much more than reading performance.

Vocabulary knowledge, or the lack thereof, impacts social interaction, participation in classroom academic routines, and learning in the content areas. In short, vocabulary knowledge is intimately connected to academic achievement in all areas, and particularly reading comprehension, for both native and nonnative English speakers (Beck, Perfetti, and McKeown 1982; Carlo, August, and Snow 2005; Nation 2001; Stahl and Nagy 2006; Elleman, Lindo Endia, Morphy, and Compton 2009).

> **Vocabulary learning can be reinforced by social interaction**
>
> see Section 3, pages 46, 61, 68

Vocabulary is also an enabling power. In my years spent living and working in a non-English-speaking country, directing the Reading Center at National–Louis University, and raising my own children, I've observed the essential role vocabulary knowledge and word awareness plays in daily life. Our students need the language and vocabulary of their home and community to be active family members and community members. They need the vocabulary of social media to fit into our technological society. They need the language and vocabulary of their interests to participate in sports, music, the arts, and other personal investigations. And, they certainly need the language and vocabulary of school to succeed, especially in their content-area classes.

The good news is that I have spent my years as a teacher researching and translating the research on vocabulary instruction into classroom instructional strategies. I have been lucky, and blessed, to be able to collaborate on a daily basis with practitioner-researchers like Char and many other excellent professionals. Besides our coauthored books (Blachowicz and Fisher 2010; Blachowicz and Cobb 2007), chapters, and articles, I have recently been engaged in a federally funded study, the Multifaceted Vocabulary Instruction Project (MCVIP) (Baumann et al. 2009–2012), which incorporated research-based best practices into elementary classrooms and which helped us identify the most useful research that teachers need to know and use.

Goals of Section 2

This section will form the link between what were identified as important issues in the previous section and the research-based instructional strategies we will describe in the following section. We will begin by sharing four essential understandings about how words are learned. These include understanding that (1) the term *vocabulary* has more than one meaning; (2) vocabulary learning requires student engagement; (3) this learning is incremental; and (4) it results from both intentional instruction and incidental learning in rich language environments.

We'll give you a historical and conceptual tour of big issues and "big names" in vocabulary research that will help us present a framework for understanding what an effective school and classroom approach to vocabulary looks like by sketching out the essential components of a vocabulary-rich curriculum and a perspective for thinking about diversifying your instruction.

We'll end this section by addressing the important questions raised by teachers in Section 1—selecting words for instruction; building

Figure 2–2   What Research Tells Us About Vocabulary Instruction

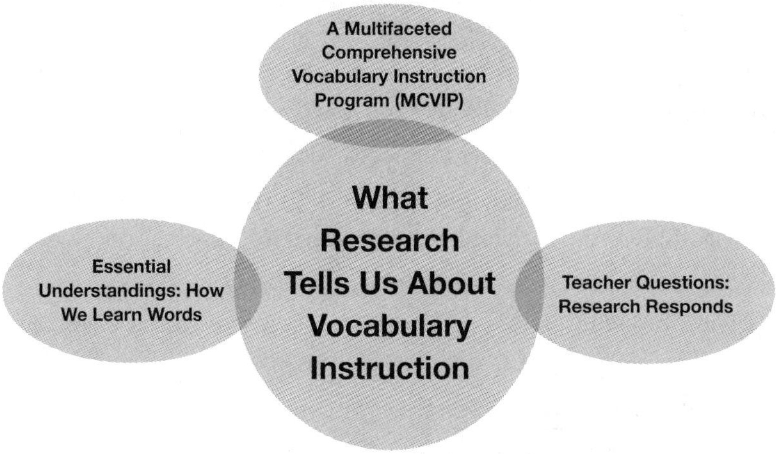

student independence; finding time to do rich instruction; and dealing with accountability and assessment. One thing we know is that graphics support comprehension; the graphic in Figure 2–2 reviews the goals of this section.

Essential Understandings: How We Learn Words

Let's begin with four essential understandings about how we learn words:

Figure 2–3

Four Essential Understandings About How We Learn Words
• Our depth of word knowledge is determined by how we use words.
• We need to have a reason to learn new words. Engagement matters.
• Words are concepts related to other words and can have multiple uses, which means that our knowledge of words can deepen.
• We learn words both through intentional instruction and incidentally.

Understanding 1: Our depth of word knowledge is defined by how we use words.

When we use the term *vocabulary*, we are referring to words (and phrases) that express something about a concept. Everyone has many types of "vocabularies." We use words in speech (oral vocabulary) that we can't decode in written text (reading vocabulary). We can recognize certain words or phrases that we understand when presented orally (listening vocabulary) but can't use those same words or phrases in speech or writing. Figure 2–4 summarizes these different types of vocabularies.

Figure 2–4 **Expressive and Receptive Vocabulary**

	Receptive (Recognition) Vocabulary	Expressive (Productive) Vocabulary
Speech	Listening vocabulary	Speaking vocabulary
Print	Reading vocabulary	Writing vocabulary

Our receptive listening vocabularies are often far advanced of our speaking, reading, or writing ones, especially in the early grades. Students might know you are talking about a dinosaur but are unable to read or write the word or use it in speech. Students' receptive vocabularies can be at least two grade levels higher than their expressive vocabularies (Biemiller and Slonim 2001). We can expand students' receptive vocabulary by reading to children from texts with more difficult vocabulary than they are using themselves. Developing expressive use of words is more difficult than receptive use. For reading or listening (receptive), students often just need a general idea of a word and use context clues—where the word appears in relation to other words (syntactic) and what the adjacent known word meaning suggests that the word means (semantic)—to help them understand. For the same word in speech or writing, students need to be given more precise meaning and practice.

In school, we want to develop all four vocabularies: oral receptive (for listening), oral expressive (for speaking), reading (receptive), and writing (expressive). So, our instruction needs to be tailored to these different kinds of vocabulary as well as to different content domains highlighted by the CCSS (National Governors Association Center for Best Practices and Council of Chief State School Officers 2010a).

We need to build students' receptive vocabulary, the ability to recognize a word when it is read or heard. Knowing a word as part of one's receptive vocabulary is usually a prerequisite for knowing it as part of one's expressive vocabulary, the more difficult ability to use the word correctly in speech and/or writing. Because the range of oral vocabularies students bring to school is so wide (Hart and Risley 1995; Graves 2006), development of oral vocabularies through read-alouds with complex texts is an important component of all elementary curricula (Marulis and Neuman 2010). We won't meet Common Core expectations of reading and writing texts of increasing complexity or the vocabulary demands they highlight across grade levels and subject areas (Blachowicz and Baumann 2013) unless we do this kind of work.

Understanding 2: We need to have a reason to learn new words. Engagement matters.

Play motivates children to learn by putting learning in a social context. Wordplay (puns, jokes, riddles, or playful games like Boggle) provides ways for teachers to foster a word-rich environment. The effectiveness of wordplay (puns, riddles, jokes, "Who is the pig who discovered relativity? Why Alber Swinestein, of course") in word learning has been proven by research (Blachowicz and Fisher 2012). Phonemic awareness (the ability to segment phonemes, such as the sound /s/ in *ambulance*), morphological awareness (getting word meaning from word part meanings such as realizing the word *reheatable* can be disambiguated into re + heat + able), and syntactic awareness (how a word functions in language—"*I saw _____ cat*" . . . *That's probably a because that is how English works*) all are part of word learning (Carlisle et al. 2010; Willows and Ryan 1986). Children develop their metalinguistic understanding of words as objects when they manipulate words in puns, combine in portmanteau words (like smoke + fog = smog),

Want ideas of how to bring fun, effective word learning into your classroom?

see Section 3, page 46

and recombine the components of words to make jokes and riddles ("What do you use to take a pig to the hospital? Why a hambulance, of course!"; Nagy and Scott 2000; Tunmer, Herriman, and Nesdale 1988). There is also evidence that students are developmentally receptive to this kind of learning and enjoy it (Johnson and Anglin 1995; Roth et al. 1996).

Students need to be given classroom time to have experiences with wordplay (more about this in Section 3). Who would not enjoy spending a few minutes each day figuring out a wuzzle (word puzzle)? That enjoyment translates to learning because wuzzles and other word games, such as those we will introduce in Section 3, demand that students think flexibly and metacognitively about words. Much of the fun stems from the fact that words can be used in multiple ways with humorous results. This gives students a sense of agency with their vocabulary. Their engagement is an indicator of their confidence in learning (Au 1997). Engagement promotes learning because it identifies a context where students can apply their learning in a knowledgeable and strategic fashion and socially interactive context (Guthrie et al. 2006). Engagement reflects the success of our instruction; it is highly correlated with achievement in all areas of literacy, including vocabulary learning (Campbell, Voelkl, and Donahue 1997).

When students see that word learning is a valuable part of the classroom culture, engagement happens. In one highly controlled study of vocabulary learning in the middle grades (Beck, Perfetti, and McKeown 1982), a curious phenomenon surfaced. Students in one classroom were learning significantly more incidental vocabulary—words no one was attempting to teach—than any of the other classrooms participating in the study. At first, the researchers were unable to identify any instruction or materials that could account for the difference. Then one researcher noted a poster of interesting words in the classroom. When the teacher was asked about it, she noted that it was the "word wall"—a place where students could write new words they encountered in reading, in conversation, on TV, or in their daily experiences. If they could write the word, talk about where they heard or saw it, and use it, they received points in a class contest; the points could be redeemed in reading or activity time. Very little expense, instructional time, or effort was involved, but the students became "tuned in" to learning new words in a way that positively affected their learning. They actively watched and listened for new words and shared them with their peers. They were motivated word learners.

Both choice and self-direction are important components of motivation. With students, especially those learning English as a second language, some degree of choice about words chosen for study is important. Jiminez (1997) found that middle school readers were more motivated and learned more vocabulary when they could have a say in selecting some of the words they were to learn. What do students say about self-directed word study? According to Ruddell and Shearer (2002), one student said, "I used to only think about vocabulary in school. The whole world is vocabulary" (352), and another stated, "I hear words everywhere that would be good to use" (352).

Self-selection does not "water down" vocabulary learning in the classroom. Fourth-grade students allowed to select their own words from a novel unit chose words of greater difficulty than graded word lists would have provided them, and they learned the words they selected (Fisher, Blachowicz, and Smith 1991). Play and choice are powerful aids to vocabulary learning as is the ability to learn vocabulary in hands-on science investigation and thematic study (Cervetti et al. 2007).

Understanding 3: Words are concepts related to other words and can have multiple uses, which means that our knowledge of words can deepen.

How can learning a word play out over time?

see Section 3, pages 43, 54, 61, 68, 72

A word's full meaning is not usually learned all at once from one exposure without context. Word knowledge is not an all-or-nothing proposition, like a switch that turns a light on or off. A better metaphor is that of a dimmer switch that gradually supplies an increasingly richer supply of light. For example, when some children first learn the word *momma* or *mama*, they apply it to all people, including men. Ultimately they narrow the meaning to their female parent and learn to use it with qualifications for others, such as "Maria's mama." In other words, learners move from not knowing a word, to being somewhat acquainted with it, to a richer, more flexible word knowledge that allows them to use new words in many modalities of expression (Graves 1986; McKeown and Beck 1988). Repeated encounters with words in a variety of oral and written contexts provide experiences and clues to the word's meaning and limitations that build over time, helping to develop and change our mental structures for a word's meaning (Eller, Pappas, and Brown 1988; Vosniadou and Ortony 1983). Meaningful use, review, and practice that calls upon students to use vocabulary in authentic ways is a "must" to develop rich and full word knowledge. Vocabulary development takes time and requires multiple encounters with words in differing contexts.

Understanding 4: We learn words through both intentional instruction and incidental means.

Estimates suggest that school-age students learn an average of 3,000–4,000 words per year (Nagy and Herman 1987; D'Anna, Zechmeister, and Hall 1991), with some researchers suggesting that this average varies widely based on the background of home and school experiences (Becker 1977; White, Graves, and Slater 1990). "Learning" in most of these studies describes growth in familiarity of recognition for certain frequent words as measured on wide-scale tests or through research studies such as those carried out for *The Living Word Vocabulary* (Dale and O'Rourke 1976) or the Text Project (Hiebert 2013).

This rapid and large growth suggests how much vocabulary learning takes place through incidental or environmental learning, including wide reading, discussion, listening, media, and firsthand experience, rather than from direct instruction. For example, students who know the word *tight end* as a position in football have

> **How can you support incidental learning?**
>
> see Section 3, page 46

typically learned that through play and experience, not from vocabulary lessons on the sport. We learn from interacting with and using words in all sorts of meaningful contexts, and it is important that the classroom supports and builds on this kind of learning.

Anne Cunningham (2005) has done an excellent summary of the research in education and psychology that underpins the aspects of wide reading (such as engagement, repeated exposure to words, rich contexts, and so forth) that are beneficial to students. Discussion in the classroom (Stahl and Vancil 1986) and around the dinner table (Snow 1991) is another way to promote incidental word learning. These studies are also supported by research on wide reading and discussion in second language learning (Pigada and Schmitt 2006). Although this type of learning through exposure cannot guarantee the learning of specific vocabulary words, it does develop a wide, flexible, and usable general vocabulary.

But vocabulary is also learned, and taught, intentionally through explicit or implicit instruction. From the popularity of *Reader's Digest's* "How to Increase Your Word Power" exercises in the 1950s and '60s to the executive word power programs advertised in airline magazines, self-study has always been part of adult self-improvement models. For school-age students, research suggests that the intentional teaching of specific words and word-learning strategies can build students' vocabularies (Tomeson and Aarnoutse 1998; Baumann et al. 2009–2012) as well as improve reading comprehension of texts containing those words (Elleman et al. 2009; Stahl and Fairbanks 1986). For students whose heritage languages are not English, or those who struggle with reading, this instruction can be even more critical (Garcia, McKoon, and August 2006). A rich language environment is critical to the vocabulary development of school-age students. With these understandings about how we learn words in place, let's move on to look at a framework for comprehensive vocabulary instruction based on these understandings.

A Framework for Comprehensive Vocabulary Instruction

The last two decades have seen an explosion of research and practical experimentation in vocabulary instruction (Wright 2012; Kame'enui and Baumann 2012; Fisher, Blachowicz, and Watts-Taffe 2011). In order to address the complex, multidimensional nature of word learning, we need to approach vocabulary comprehensively (Stahl and Nagy 2006; Lubliner and Smetana 2005; Watts-Taffe, Blachowicz, and Fisher 2009) and this leads us to some key instructional guidelines that are critical to planning and delivering excellent vocabulary instruction (Graves 2006):

- providing rich and varied language experiences
- fostering word consciousness
- teaching word-learning strategies
- teaching individual words

These components of a comprehensive vocabulary program were validated by Baumann and his associates in the MCVIP and resulted in significant gains by upper elementary students on standardized and performance measures (Baumann et al. 2011; Graves 2006; Blachowicz and Baumann 2012).

Figure 2–5 MCVIP Comprehensive Model

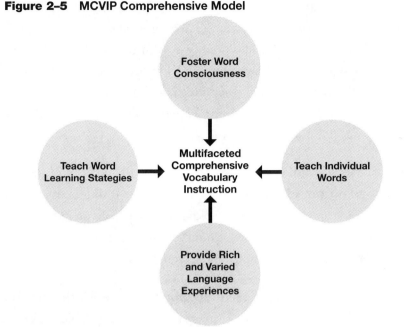

Providing Rich and Varied Language Experiences

Students need to be immersed in a language-rich environment to build oral vocabulary (Hart and Risley 1995). They learn words incidentally by reading independently (Cunningham 2005; Kim and White 2008); through exposure to enriched oral language that comes from listening to and reading well-written text, media, and classroom discourse; by participating in conversation and discussion where they learn the conventions of conversational talk; as well as by talking with peers to solve problems and complete tasks and presentational talking to share ideas before the group (Johnston 2004). They also learn words in the texts of increasing complexity that they read in school (Hiebert and Cervetti 2009).

Read aloud from stimulating texts with rich vocabulary. These read-alouds can be from materials that students would not be able to read themselves but that they can understand and should include discussion in which carefully chosen vocabulary can be highlighted during or after reading. We also know that students acquire vocabulary in an accelerated fashion through read-alouds when teachers, peers, or caregivers provide elaboration on words in the texts (van Kleeck, Stahl, and Bauer 2003; Blachowicz and Obrochta 2005, 2007; Beck, McKeown, and Kucan 2008; Biemiller and Boote 2006). Interactive read-aloud experiences and word explanations promote students' learning and retention of new words.

Promote incidental word learning through classroom independent reading time and support. Students need time and support for regular personal reading of on-level texts. Teachers can model book selection and do book talks to stimulate interest in different genres, authors, and formats (electronic texts, manga, etc.).

Develop students' expressive vocabulary through discussion and writing. Provide time and support for meaningful student discussion and writing. Students need to receive modeling and support for *how* to talk about a text or issue (Evans 2002). This support may be as basic as turn taking, looking at the speaker, and giving some sort of response, or more elaborate support in discussion, such as PRC2 (Ogle and Correa 2010) or using vocabulary frames (Blachowicz, Bates, and Cieply 2012) or charting for character traits (Manyak 2007). We will elaborate on all of these in Section 3. Similarly, when writing, students need to be supported with graphics, planning, and other models to begin using elaborated vocabulary.

Fostering Word Consciousness

Word consciousness is a term used to describe a variety of students' cognitive and metacognitive knowledge and behaviors with respect to vocabulary. These include awareness of when a word's meaning is understood and when it is not; knowledge of the morphological, etymological, and interrelational aspects of words; appreciation of figurative language and language play; and recognition that interesting, colorful words can be used effectively in oral and written communication (Blachowicz et al. 2006; Graves and Watts-Taffe 2002; Scott, Miller, and Flinspach 2012).

There have been several studies conducted by Scott and colleagues documenting the impact of word consciousness instruction and environments on students' affective and cognitive growth in vocabulary (Scott et al. 2008; Scott et al. 2009; Scott, Flinspach, and Vevea 2011). To build word consciousness teachers need to motivate students through engaging and playful means, develop their appreciation of fine writing in both fictional and informational text, teach them about the ways words work for effect such as in figurative language, and support them in careful and nuanced selection of words for their own talk and writing.

Teaching Word-Learning Strategies

Students can be taught to infer the meanings of unknown or partially known words by using context clues and analyzing root words, prefixes and suffixes, and Latin and Greek word roots. These are sometimes called "meta-strategies" because they focus on manipulating word parts. Several recent studies document that morphemic analysis enhances students' ability to learn new words independently (Baumann et al. 2011; Baumann et al. 2003; Baumann et al. 2002); these studies support teaching meta-strategies to grade-level readers (Bowers, Kirby, and Deacon 2010; Carlisle et al. 2010), as well as to students who experience reading difficulties (Goodwin and Ahn 2010; Reed 2008). The most effective instruction goes beyond the ways context and word parts work and focuses on how to *apply* these clues when reading.

Teaching Individual Words

There is considerable research support for teaching students the meanings of words directly through a variety of strategies and techniques (Beck and McKeown 1991; Blachowicz and Fisher 2010; Graves 2009), many of which we will share with you in Section 3. Often, during reading or study, a word comes up that teachers need to teach in real time, quickly, and move on with whatever content or language lesson is going on.

For a simple, individual word lesson (Beck, McKeown, and Kucan 2008; Baumann et al. 2009–2012) to introduce students to new words, we know that the following steps work well.

Teaching and Individual Word Instructional Strategy
- Make sure the students see the word and can pronounce it.
- Give or generate a "kid-friendly" definition for the term.
- Present an oral or written context using visuals or objects when possible to flesh out the context.
- Ask students for a semantic response. For example, *Would you invite a burglar into your home? Why or why not?*
- Have students use words in speech and writing.

This process is an efficient way to teach vocabulary that can be handily connected to students' prior knowledge (we give examples in Section 3). Ideally this is only a first step followed by connecting the individual words to a network of related words within their content area or thematic unit area of study. However, for a more complex term, like *democracy*, which we use as an example in Section 3, different instruction is called for, which is why we now move on to talk about teacher decision making for flexible instruction.

Flexible instruction means that you, the individual teacher, make some important choices, but it's not as hard as it may sound

you'll see how in Section 3

The Need for Flexible Instruction
Our four components from the MCVIP study provide us with our curriculum goals for comprehensive vocabulary instruction. We have a three-word mnemonic for different forms of vocabulary teaching—"Flood, Fast, Focus"—to help our teachers consider the choices they have to make in implementing the framework we presented (Blachowicz, Bates, and Cieply 2013).

Flood. First, we emphasize that not all learning requires intentional teacher-directed instruction; you need to consciously flood your classroom with words related to your topic of study, not all of which you want your students to learn to the same depth. Nagy, Herman, and Anderson (1985) point out that there is no way we can intentionally teach all the words students learn each year. An enriched environment that increases the meaningful and interesting encounters students have with words can increase this incidental learning (Cunningham 2005). Wide reading and intensive writing are part and parcel of the flood of words. Students can create word blasts or semantic maps (Pittelman et al. 1991) and engage in sorting and other activities to begin building a relational set of terms related to your topic of study (Blachowicz and Fisher 2010). Thematic instruction and content-area study provide the topical reference points for building these networks of related terms and also provide the natural repetition of words in varied contexts necessary for learning (Hiebert and Kamil 2005).

Because the number of encounters needed to learn a word depends on learner characteristics such as background experience and knowledge, interest, engagement and motivation, characteristics of the words to be learned (such as concreteness or abstractness), and contextual characteristics, there is no definitive research that can be cited to answer the question, "Well, how many repetitions are needed?" Infant and toddler learning studies and studies of foreign language learners report ranges for ten to forty encounters for infants and toddlers as necessary (Bergelson and Swingley 2013) and six to twenty repetitions for older second language learners (Pigada and Schmitt 2006). Yet other studies suggest "fast mapping": making an initial inference about the meaning of a word in only one or two encounters (Medina et al. 2011). (Perhaps this is how our children and students learn all those forbidden words so fast!) Our observational research on fourth- and fifth-grade classrooms implementing Flood in a comprehensive model along with Fast and Focus instruction (noted below) documented more than twenty-five observed encounters with target words over a one-week period. And these were only times when we heard the words highlighted orally or in discussion with the group, or encountered in assigned reading or review during our one-hour daily observations. It did not include any encounters with the words when we were not present or in student individual work, reading, writing, or homework (Blachowicz, Bates, and Cieply 2013). It should be noted that these are meaningful and varied encounters for the students, not rote repetitions of a definition.

Self-selection of words for personal word books personalizes and individualizes the Flood words for each student. Research on self-selection (Fisher et al. 1991; Haggard 1982) reveals that students can select some of their own words for personal word books or word walls to begin recording their own interesting words for study, often choosing words more difficult than the teacher or text list would suggest. In our study, students learned 64 to 75 percent of the words they selected (Fisher et al. 1991). Self-selection differentiates for your students with more prior knowledge, and it also allows students who are just building a basic vocabulary to choose the words that are right for them. You can have as many Flood words as you want in a class to enrich the environment, but these are not assigned to all or tested in traditional ways. Rather, they form a backdrop of topically related terms for incidental learning.

Fast. You can use Fast instruction, which we introduced above in our discussion of Intentional "Teaching Individual Words" for terms where an easy definition or analogy will build on knowledge the students already have. We know that short definitional word explanations can do the trick when the concept is familiar but the term is not (Kame'enui et al. 1982; McKeown et al. 1985; Pany, Jenkins, and Schreck 1982; Baumann et al. 2003). Fast-paced instruction identifies the word, provides a synonym, gives an example of use, and then asks students to provide their own connection or synonym. When words are *almost* alike, a short feature analysis, word laddering, or semantic decision question ("Would you be more scared by a huge or gigantic monster?") can help establish these word nuances.

Focus. Use Focus instruction for words where deeper, semantically rich teaching of a new concept is required, such as the word *democracy,* which we will elaborate on in Section 3. This is an easy word to memorize a definition for, but it represents a rich and complex topic that continues to grow in a network of meaning we refine as we move more and more into a global society. This demands instruction that involves both definitional and contextual information, multiple exposures, close reading in many contexts, and deep levels of processing, calling on students to discuss and use the word with teacher and peers, so that students develop a rich base for word meaning (Mezynski 1983; Graves 1986; Nagy and Scott 2000; Stahl and Fairbanks 1986) and reading comprehension (Baumann 2009; Elleman et al. 2009).

These three dimensions (Flood, Fast, Focus) can help you fine-tune instruction. You need to choose whether a word can be taught easily or whether it needs more instruction. Imagine a group of fourth-grade students who are familiar with the term *crown.* Teaching the meaning of the word *diadem* won't be too difficult. They already have the concept of a crown and are learning only a new label for a related term. Little, if any, instruction might be needed, though teaching methods for ensuring repetition through reading and use (Fast instruction) can help the word stick. For the same students, in the same selection, the word *nostalgia,* however, would probably be harder to teach. This is an abstract concept that might not be too familiar to most nine-year-olds, and the teacher would have to help the student, through rich discussion and work with the words (Focus instruction), to establish a rich network of related concepts, such as *longing, the past,* and so forth. So it makes sense to think about "knowing" a word as a continuous process that can be affected by meaningful encounters with words and by instruction aimed at helping the learner develop a network of understanding. The instructional situation that the teacher selects will vary depending both on the frameworks of knowledge the learners already have and the importance of the term to the task at hand.

Teacher Questions: Research Responds

As Char explained in Section 1, teachers have four common questions about vocabulary instruction. In Section 1, you read common responses and some challenges to those assumptions. Now, you'll learn how research has answered these questions.

Word Selection: How do I select words and when should I teach them?

From research by Nagy and others that we discussed earlier, we know that intentional instruction cannot account for all the words students learn. For that reason, classrooms should be flooded with words related to topics of study and ways to create related sets of these words so that maximal incidental learning can take place.

However, teachers know students have a right to receive Fast and Focus instruction on key content vocabulary but sometimes feel unsure about selecting the most important vocabulary to teach. While there is no research to support any single way for selecting words for instruction, Beck, McKeown, and Kucan (2008) have been leaders in promoting the idea of what they have called *three tiers of word importance* to help in this process. What they label Tier 3 words are the unfamiliar content-area concepts (e.g., *photosynthesis*) that need extended time and effort for instruction in conjunction with their content classes. Their Tier 2 words are new labels for established concepts (e.g., *petal*), and Tier 1 words are the most basic words (*flower, leaf*) that usually do not require instruction in school for students who are comfortable with English as the language of instruction. They suggest that teachers focus on Tier 2 words that can be used across many contexts.

Other suggestions for choice include using a map of the story or text structure as a guide for selecting key words for study (see examples in Section 3 of Vocab-o-gram and Democracy Frayer Model map; Blachowicz and Fisher 2010), or using words chosen by frequency in text (Fry and Rasinski 2007). Choosing content words can be facilitated by the textual materials that are used in many classrooms—boldface, highlighting, and glossaries help with this selection process. The frequency of occurrence of term and its use in diagrams, figures, and labeling also provide a clue to word or phrase importance.

Baumann and Graves provide a model for selecting math vocabulary.

First, identify the domain-specific words at an appropriate level (e.g., a middle school math teacher would work from Marzano and Pickering's Level 3 math list, which correspond to grades 6–8).

Second, identify words deemed to be important for instruction (e.g., words from the Level 3 math list that appear in the adopted math textbook, curriculum, or state standards).

Third, select words for instruction by asking "Is this term critically important to the mathematics content I will be teaching this year?"

Fourth, organize the selected words according to how they occur in your curriculum. (2010, 8)

We would amplify this example by suggesting that the words be separated into words that are amenable to Fast instruction because they are established concepts and words that need Focus instruction because the underlying concept is difficult and unfamiliar. To cross-check, teachers can use word lists such as Marzano and Pickering's (2005) or Hiebert's (2013) to help them in constructing lists of semantically related words (Marvey, Dunlosky, and Schwartz 2006), which recognize the later usefulness of content words to curricular and life needs. Finally, we note that this selection process is aided greatly by teamwork across grades and articulation with the grades above and below your own.

Teachers often ask, "How many words should I teach?" Again, like research on the number of repetitions needed for school-age students to learn a word, this is a question that has no firm research-based answer. Research on vocabulary intervention programs (Beck and McKeown 2007; Marzano and Pickering 2005; Snow, Lawrence, and White 2009) worked with a range of 100–250 words per year, or 3–6 words a week. Biemiller (2005) suggests 1,000 words per year, which works out to about 25–30 words a week, though these are words for primary students, many of which are already in a child's oral vocabulary. In our study of student self-selection (Fisher, Blachowicz, and Smith 1991), which we discussed earlier, student groups selected over 75 words for study for a three-week period. In helping us develop our process of Flood, Fast, and Focus, our teachers settled on a number of 8–12 important words per week as a "doable" number to be followed up on with weekly review and assessment (Blachowicz, Bates, and Cieply 2010). These were a mix of content-area and language arts words that the teachers decided should be "everybody" words, words each child deserved to know. One teacher noted, "I know that they have many more words in their personal word books that they learned, but these are 'take-home' and assessed words for everybody, which they need to show they can use in speech and writing."

Independence: How can I help my students become independent word learners?

As students move into and through the upper elementary grades, they should be developing in their responsibility for their own learning. Instruction in word-learning strategies, which we noted earlier, is one way to build independence. We have also discussed student self-selection and choice of personal words for study to augment the "everybody" words the teacher selects for Focus instruction. As students become more savvy about text features and other cues to important vocabulary in different domains, such as frequency, typography, common morphological parts, and so forth, they can begin to create their own lists for study. Similarly, students can learn to work in teams to share and develop knowledge for their classmates as well as across grades in their school.

Last, students can apply and augment their interest and skill with traditional references and with technological references and search processes to develop the ability to use tools for independent learning. Dictionaries can be viewed as another tool for word learning. Studies of students from elementary grades through college indicate that many have trouble interpreting definitional language (McKeown 1985; Nist and Olejnik 1995). For the dictionary to be an effective component in a learner's vocabulary development, some attention needs to be paid to helping students learn to use the information in a dictionary and to providing them with dictionaries with "kid-friendly definitions." A large number of "learner's dictionaries" (see Section 3 for a list) can make these tools more accessible to students. While this book is meant to present alternatives to looking up a list of words, we believe reference resources are important to all learners and technology is a gigantic tool for searching for and clarifying meaning (Watts-Taffe and Gwinn 2007).

Time: How do I find time for meaningful vocabulary instruction?

In our project classrooms (Baumann et al. 2009–2012), one way our teachers found time for vocabulary instruction was by making it an integral part of their comprehension instruction. Some of the strategies we will share in Section 3 are "all-in-one" approaches that use vocabulary as before, during, and after keys to comprehension. Remembering that vocabulary learning is incremental removes the need to front-load all your vocabulary work at the beginning of a lesson, which is not the most effective way to help words stick.

Another way our teachers find time for vocabulary is by making it part of every content class rather than overloading the language arts curriculum. As you will see in Section 3, content-area instruction is a natural for morphology and other word strategy instruction. It also spreads the load of vocabulary teaching and learning. Content classes are thematic and topicalized by nature, so the vocabulary is presented in related sets, a practice substantiated as effective by research with both learners whose first language is English and English as a second language learners. Research by Durso and Coggins (1991) found evidence that organizing vocabulary words during word study facilitated performance in vocabulary tasks when compared with word study of the same words presented without organization, a finding seconded in English language learner research of Marvey, Dunlosky, and Schwartz (2006).

All of these time-saving approaches are very consistent with current CCSS (National Governors Association Center for Best Practices and Council of Chief State School Officers 2010a) approaches to integrating vocabulary with the general curriculum. This question also relates directly to the one that follows, as giving students more choice and responsibility can be a time-saver for the teacher as well as help develop student independence.

Assessment: How can I assess and hold students accountable?

Objective tests focus on receptive recognition vocabulary and, as such, are useful for a low-level assessment of vocabulary. These can be fine-tuned a bit more by constructing maze or cloze assessments, passages with words omitted with or without choices, which add context to the mix. Many teachers like pre- and postassessments to look at student growth over a unit.

Building a routine of regular, engaging review was cited by teachers in our study as one way of ensuring student accountability (Blachowicz, Bates, and Cieply 2010). Students participated in a weekly review of "everybody words" and were asked to "show what you know" each week in written assignments and oral presentations, which they documented in vocabulary notebooks as ways of consolidating their learning. Student writing with targeted vocabulary and oral presentation provides two ways to assess expressive vocabulary, and their own personal word books or content dictionaries can also be examined with a rubric for assessment.

The assessment designers working on CCSS assessment (Partnership for Assessment of College and Career Readiness [PARCC]; Smarter Balanced) are also developing assessments that have more sensitive ways of looking at the development of independent word-learning strategies. These call on students to supply evidence from the text for their use of context and other clues. These and other ideas will be fleshed out in Section 3.

Moving from Understanding to Practice

In Section 1 we sketched out some of the dilemmas and limiting factors teachers face in enacting thoughtful vocabulary instruction. In this section, we connected some of those issues to research that grounds our understandings of the nature of vocabulary and the school curriculum, research that helps us with thorny questions. Now on to Section 3 and the ideas we have collected and field-tested to share with you as you go beyond "list and look up" into more sophisticated instruction.

SECTION 3

BUT THAT

Flexible Instruction for
Vocabulary Learning

CAMILLE BLACHOWICZ and **CHARLENE COBB**

We know we can do better than putting word lists on the board and asking students to look them up. We've shared the research that tells us how and why, so now let's get into the nitty-gritty of what the practices look like in the classroom. Vocabulary learning needs to happen in a variety of ways over an extended period of time. We need to maximize students' opportunities for incidental learning as well as support word learning through intentional explicit and implicit instruction. In this section, we will help you plan comprehensive vocabulary instruction for your students. As explained in Section 2, effective vocabulary instruction starts with four essential understandings related to depth of knowledge, engagement, the conceptual basis of word knowledge, and both intentional and incidental learning. We connected these to practice by proposing four essential components of a good vocabulary program that have been supported by and developed through research.

Figure 3–1 Connecting Understanding to Practice

Because we understand that vocabulary instruction needs to

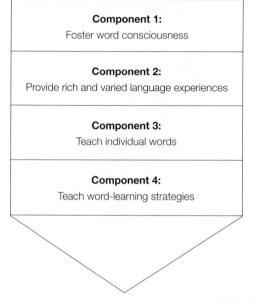

Component 1:
Foster word consciousness

Component 2:
Provide rich and varied language experiences

Component 3:
Teach individual words

Component 4:
Teach word-learning strategies

We give students a variety of experiences with words over time, adapting our approach to instruction, depending on students' needs and experience with a word.

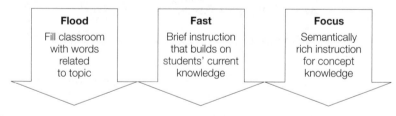

Flood
Fill classroom with words related to topic

Fast
Brief instruction that builds on students' current knowledge

Focus
Semantically rich instruction for concept knowledge

We provide students with opportunities to demonstrate their learning

Engaging Review ⟺ Accountability (Assessment)

In Section 2, Camille explained that a word's meaning is not usually learned all at once. She used the metaphor of a dimmer switch to describe how the light, or understanding, of a word's meaning, increases over time. The metaphor applies to our vocabulary instruction as well:

We need to choose the intensity of our instruction based on students' needs. There is a framework that informs our instruction called "Flood, Fast, and Focus." See Figure 3–1 for a section organizer.

Fostering Word Consciousness

Take a moment to evaluate existing evidence of word consciousness in your classroom environment, yourself, and your students. Teachers helped us develop the self-analysis tool shown in Figure 3–2 as part of our Multifaceted Comprehensive Instruction (MCVIP) professional development project we shared with you in Section 2 (Baumann et al. 2009–2012). Use it to help you think about the things you do well in your classroom and the areas where you could use some new ideas. If you can't check off some of the items, don't worry. In this section, we'll show you what to do so that you can.

Figure 3–2 Evidence of Word Consciousness in Classroom Environment, Teacher, and Students

---

Analyze Your Vocabulary Environment

1. My classroom shows physical signs of word consciousness. You can see . . .

   ___ word charts or word walls (showing student input) used and changed regularly

   ___ books, including those on words, wordplay, specialized and learner dictionaries, dictionaries (where students can easily access them)

   ___ labels in classroom

   ___ word games

   ___ puzzle books and software

   ___ student-made word books, alphabet books, dictionaries, computer files, PowerPoint displays, SMART Board lessons

---

2. As a teacher, I show enthusiasm for language, words, and word learning.

___ I read aloud daily from materials with a little more challenging vocabulary than my students can read on their own.

___ I engage students daily in at least one playful word activity.

___ I understand differences and connections between spelling, phonics, and vocabulary, and focus on meaning each day.

___ If asked, my students would say their teacher loves words and wordplay.

___ I keep myself updated with journals and websites on vocabulary.

3. My students show enthusiasm for words and word learning. They . . .

___ have personal dictionaries or word logs

___ can use a dictionary and other references on an appropriate level

___ have a strategy for dealing with unknown words

___ spend part of each day reading independently

___ can name a favorite wordbook, puzzle activity, and/or word game

___ use new vocabulary in talk, discussion, writing, and presentation

___ enjoy and share new words, word games, puns, riddles, wordplay

To set the stage for developing students' word consciousness, we need to *flood* students with words. Word consciousness also includes teaching students about how words work so that they can be better, more interesting, and more precise readers, speakers, and writers. Let's start with revisiting some of the Flood strategies related to the explanations we introduced in Section 2.

Stock the Classroom with Engaging Books

Even if you have an excellent school library, your classroom should have a library of interesting books and magazines for students to pick up whenever time permits. Make sure that it includes books on words and wordplay:

- Homophones, such as Fred Gwynne's *The King Who Rained* (Aladdin, 1988)
- Puns, jokes, and riddles, such as those by Mike Thayer
- Specialized vocabulary like:

    A Rattle of Bones, written and illustrated by Kipling West (Orchard, 1999)

    Gobble: The Complete Book of Thanksgiving Words, by Lynda Graham-Barber, illustrated by Betsy Lewin (Avon Camelot, 1993)

    Mushy! The Complete Book of Valentine Words, by Lynda Graham-Barber, illustrated by Betsy Lewin (Simon and Schuster Children's, 1991; Avon Camelot, 1993)

You can find word books for almost any holiday or interest. And don't forget specialized dictionaries such as *HipHoptionary: A Dictionary of Hip-Hop Terms* (Westbrook, 2002). Many of these can be found on Internet bookstores (such as Amazon) with dictionaries of everything from BMX bikes to ballet!

Why is wordplay important?

see Section 2, pages 23–24

Play Games

The five most popular classroom word games are Bananagrams, Apples to Apples, Taboo, Scrabble, and Boggle, each of which has a junior version. Your students can find additional games on the Fun with Words website (www.fun-with-words.com). Encourage your school library to have a set of word games at various levels that can be checked out for the classroom or for home.

Use Every Moment

Students should always have three books at their desk to choose among whenever they have a few extra minutes: one "just-right" book at their instructional level, one easy book they can cruise through (or an old favorite to reread), and one challenging book on a topic of very high interest. Middle schoolers who change classes can keep a paperback in their backpack at all times for those moments when they are waiting for a class to begin.

Let Students Choose

It's important to let your students choose some of their own words to learn and record in their own way and take responsibility for their learning. Entering new and interesting words in a word book and sharing them in weekly "word expert" sessions is a great way for students to develop their vocabulary and their interest in words and word learning. The "word square" recording format (four boxes surrounding the key word) includes both visual and verbal pegs on which to hang a word's meaning. Students provide dictionary definitions and also define the term in their own words; then students give a personal use of the word and draw or paste in a visual reminder of the word's meaning (see Figure 3–3).

Teach How Words Work

Another aspect of being word conscious is knowing how words work so we can understand new words by relating them to ones we know, appreciate author's choices, and make careful word selections when we write. Asking students to find new ways to replace overworked words like *good* and *nice* is another way of teaching them the basis for synonyms, which is a term describing a type of word relationships of words that mean the same, or almost the same, thing. Like synonyms, these categories of word relationships (see Figure 3–4) are interesting as well as essential for developing a mature, interconnected, and varied vocabulary.

Figure 3–3 Example of a Student Word Square

Context The candle illuminated the dark corners of the room.	Definition to provide or brighten with light Definition in my own words: light up; make clearer or brighter
illuminate (verb)	
Personal use The light illuminated the book I was trying to read.	Drawings or graphics that illustrate the meaning

Figure 3–4 Basic Word Relationship Categories

Category	Definition	Examples
Synonym*	Words that are the same or nearly the same in meaning	*fight*, *quarrel*, *argument*, *squabble*, *altercation*, *beef*, *feud*, *brawl*, *fray*, *scuffle*
Antonym*	Words that are opposite or nearly opposite in meaning	*hot/cold*; *night/ day*; *warm/chilly*; *boisterous* (*loud*)/ *placid* (*quiet*)
Homonym	Words that have the same spelling and pronunciation but different meanings	*left* (the opposite direction of right)/*left* (past tense of *leave*, "to go away from")
Homophone	Words with the same pronunciation but different spellings and meanings	*night, knight* *rode, road, rowed*

Homograph*	Words with the same spelling but different meanings and sometimes different pronunciations	*tear* in my eye/*tear* in my shirt a *bow* tie/take a *bow* *conduct* the band/ have good *conduct*
Denotation*	The most basic or dictionary meaning of a word	My brother sometimes *misbehaves*. The old sandwich did not look *appetizing*.
Connotation*	An emotional or imaginative meaning of a word	My brother is a *brat*. The old sandwich was *disgusting* to look at.
Alliteration*	Repeating the beginning sounds of words	Five famished foxes feasted on fifty fresh fish.
Simile*	Comparing two different things using the words *like* or *as*	*Ann* runs like a *deer*. The *cookie* was as hard as a *rock*.
Metaphor*	Comparing words or ideas in a figurative way without using *like* or *as*	*Ann* is a *deer* when she runs. The stale *cookie* was a *rock*.
Hyperbole*	An exaggerated statement	Tommy ate a ton of pizza. It took me a million years to clean my room.
Idiom*	A saying that does not mean the same as the individual words	It's raining cats and dogs. Now you'll be in hot water.

Figure 3–4 (*continues*)

Figure 3–4 (*continued*)

Acronym	Abbreviations using the first letters of words	USA = United States of America ATM = automatic teller machine SCUBA = self-contained underwater breathing apparatus
Personification*/ Anthropomorphism	Attaching human qualities to animals, ideas, or things	The kite danced in the wind. The stars are winking at us.

*Categories called for in the Common Core State Standards

For students in grades 3–8, word relationship categories can be enriched to include instruction of more complex words such as oxymorons, spoonerisms, and others. Instruction that includes these categories of words (Figure 3–5) is engaging and enjoyable for students.

Figure 3–5   Complex Word Relationship Categories

Category	Definition	Example
Slang	Informal words added to our language	*chopper* (helicopter), *hacker* (computer intruder), *24/7* (all day, every day), *junk food* (fast food)
Oxymoron*	Using words together that have opposite or very different meanings	Mom believes in *tough love.* Please grab me some *plastic silverware.*
Onomatopoeia	A word that imitates a noise or an action	*buzz, achoo, bubble, fizz*

Pun*	A joke based on different possible meanings of a word or the fact that there are words that sound alike but have different meanings	Q. What do you call a train who sneezes? A. Achoo-choo train
Tom Swifty	A phrase that includes a kind of joke or play on words (a pun)	"I need to *sharpen my pencil*," said Anne *bluntly*. "Haven't you *finished knitting* that sock yet?" Mom *needled*.
Spoonerism	A comical phrase resulting from the switching of initial consonants	"Please pass the salt and shecker papers."
Palindrome	Words or phrases that read the same backward as forward	*mom*, *dad*, *pop*
Portmanteau/ Combined Word	A word formed by blending two other words	*brunch* is a combination of *breakfast* and *lunch*
Borrowed/ Loan Word	Words from another language commonly used in English	*latte*, *taco*, *beret*
Collective Noun	Word used to define a group	a herd of sheep; a gaggle of geese
Anagram	Words made by rearranging the letters of another word	*stop* is an anagram of *pots*
Riddle	Generally a question that takes clever or unexpected thinking to answer	Q. What has four wheels and flies? A. A garbage truck
Hink Pink	Riddles whose answer is a pair of rhyming words	Q. What do you call a chubby kitty? A. A fat cat

*Categories called for in the Common Core State Standards

These word relationship categories make great topics for a daily 3 ×
5 (Blachowicz and Fisher 2010), which is taking three minutes a day,
five days a week to discuss, give, and ask for examples related to your
word category of the week. Then encourage students to watch for the
words in reading, discussions, and TV and to use them in their writing.
Making collection bulletin boards is an easy way to emphasize one or
two of these a month and can build more word-conscious speakers,
readers, and writers.

Teaching Individual Words

It's important to introduce words to students in ways that are engaging and promote thought and discussion. "Fast" teaching, in which
one exposes students to sets of words in the context of thoughtful
activities, is often the first step in looking at the vocabulary related
to a selection, section, or unit. When reading text closely, students
can be supported in working through selected word meanings as they
read. This works well for words that are explained or clued by context.
For other vocabulary, however, presentation is called for. The rule of
thumb is "Leave 'em needing more." By this we mean, don't make
this presentation a substitute for reading. Make it a preliminary to
reading, inquiry, and deeper study.

Explanatory Example

For example, Monica, a fifth-grade teacher, knows her students will
encounter labels for a number of other forms of government during a
unit on democracy. Because she knows they understand the idea of a
head of the country (the words *king* and *queen* are very familiar), she
has an easy anchor for some fast teaching. She puts the chart in Figure
3–6 on her SMART Board with only the first column filled in, gives
each student a blank paper copy, and Fast teaches each word using
the MCVIP guidelines discussed in Section 2 for teaching individual
words. Important steps in this process are for students to

- See and pronounce the word.
- Hear the word in context.
- Receive a definition (either from the teacher or another student).
- Make a connection with how they might use the word.

Students begin by filling in a blank chart with the words as they are recorded on the SMART Board and pronounced by Monica.

Starting with *president*, Monica helps students create their own scaffold for reading by using their input wherever possible to construct a kid-friendly definition and share some brief examples. (She skips *dictator* and *matriarch*, which are well explained in the text.) She keeps this overview to ten minutes or less and then has students use the chart to help them during reading. This is Fast presentation.

Later, she will have students complete their individual charts after reading the text section that discusses each term including determining the entries for *dictator* and *matriarch* from their reading. They have a final discussion and create a class chart from their individual contributions (see Figure 3–7).

Figure 3–6 Initial Chart for Fast Teaching the Labels of Forms of Government

A . . .	Definition is a/an . . .	is head of a . . .	Example	Notes
president		democracy		
monarch		monarchy		
dictator		dictatorship		
matriarch		matriarchy		
plutocrat		plutocracy		

Figure 3–7 Final Class Chart During Discussion of the Labels of Forms of Government

A . . .	Definition is a/an . . .	is head of a . . .	Example	Notes
president	elected head of a country	democracy	President Obama of the U.S.	Important to know
monarch	hereditary ruler	monarchy	Queen Elizabeth of England	Important to know

This chart can be amplified with some extra columns for student notes, authors' uses of the terms, and created pictures or graphics as they continue on with the unit. Other ways to Fast teach vocabulary include analogies (*President Obama is to democracy as* _____ *is to* _____), synonym webs, and word maps. We also like semantic word sorts.

Semantic Word Sorts

Word sorts engage students physically as well as mentally and prompt them to explore the relationships between and among words. Word sorts use a group of semantically related words that are essential and important to a unit of instruction. Students are given the words in random order and asked to organize or classify them. As a before-reading strategy, the students are asked to develop their own categories. This is also referred to as an *open word sort*.

Lupe is a fourth-grade teacher beginning a unit on geometry. Her students' third-grade curriculum included learning to identify two-dimensional figures (rhombus, rectangle, square, quadrilateral), and the Common Core standards for geometry require that fourth graders "draw and identify lines and angles, and classify shapes by properties of their lines and angles" (CCSS/Math/Content/4.G.A. 1–3; National Governors Association Center for Best Practices and Council of Chief State School Officers 2010a).

Lupe wants to know if her students learned the words that were part of their third-grade instruction last year (*rhombus, rectangle, square, quadrilateral*) and also help her students set a purpose for their learning. She gives each student the set of words shown in Figure 3–8. Lupe reads the words aloud to the students, because some words may be in students' listening vocabulary but not in their reading vocabulary. After reading the words aloud, Lupe asks the students to cut the words apart and then group the words to show how they are related to one another. She reminds students that there may be more than one way to organize the words and also that they will be required to explain their groupings.

Figure 3–8 Math Vocabulary

Directions: Sort these words into groups of at least two. Be prepared to explain your thinking.		
rhombus	*angles*	*rays*
rectangle	*parallel*	*quadrilateral*
acute	*right*	*perpendicular*
segments	*square*	*obtuse*
lines		

As students sort, Lupe walks about the room, occasionally stopping to speak with a student. She asks Alicia, "Tell me why you have *square, quadrilateral, right*, and *parallel* together?" Alicia explains, "Well, a square is a quadrilateral with right angles, and parallel lines." Lupe says to Jorge, "Explain why you have *square, rhombus, rectangle*, and *quadrilateral* sorted together." Jorge responds, "They are all kinds of shapes." Alicia is thinking about the features of a figure; Jorge is categorizing figures.

After a few minutes, Lupe tells the class, "I noticed words being sorted in several ways. I want you to share your thinking, so turn and talk with your table partner. Explain how and why you sorted your words." After a few more minutes, she asks partners to turn and talk with another set of partners. Each group of four then reports to the whole class how and why their sorts were similar or different, until everyone understands the various classification systems that can be applied to the same set of words. This discussion, which gives the students the opportunity to use the designated math terms orally, is especially important for Lupe's English language learners. It also gives students a chance to define the terms in their own words. At the same time, it gives Lupe an idea of how to adjust her instruction to ensure that all students will be able to meet the standard. She follows up this introductory activity by teaching individual words that need clarification.

All of these quick presentations can help give students a first taste of the vocabulary they will further develop through reading and through rich and varied language experiences.

Fostering Rich and Varied Language Experiences

James Britton (1987) said it beautifully when he noted that reading and writing "float on a sea of talk" (16). Attention to developing and using rich language is necessary for all the teaching we do. As we noted in Section 2, engaging students in varied types of talk (Ogle 2007), conversational, problem solving, and presentational, is essential for building both comprehension and the vocabulary that supports it (Hart and Risley 1995). The Flood ideas we presented earlier exposed and helped students encounter and use a variety of words and types of language in books and the environment. However, some words are more difficult to teach because the concepts they refer to are complex. These often require a combination of Fast and Focus instruction and call on students to engage in rich talk and extensive reading and writing.

For example, in a unit on *democracy*, this key term is an abstract concept with many features that may differ slightly from country to country. A Fast way to start would be with presenting a relational set to topicalize the word.

Charting and Mapping Relational Sets

Building relational sets of words helps students focus on a topic. Charting and mapping these words makes the relationship graphic. Figure 3–9 is a map of words related to democracy. This is the simplest form of a semantic map, a topical map, which groups words around a central organizing feature. It's a "starter" map; the exact meanings of the other words are not essential at this point but the words have been assigned a category, which will be helpful when they are next encountered in text or speech. Later, each word can be elaborated upon in more articulated semantic graphics.

Figure 3–9 Topical Map of Words Related to Democracy

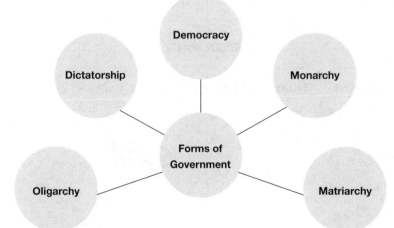

Democracy is a concept that needs to be developed through reading and rich discussion. As they read through their texts in social studies, view media, and conduct independent research, students focus on the word *democracy*, creating a more elaborated word square over time as a way to record and scaffold class discussion (see Figure 3–10). This word square is a form of semantic map (Pittelman et al. 1991). You may have heard it referred to as a Frayer Model or Concept of Definition Frame (Frayer et al. 1969; Schwartz and Raphael 1985). All of these have extensive research showing their effectiveness in conceptual and vocabulary development.

Figure 3–10 **Example of a Frayer Model Word Square**

Definition: a government by the people exercised either through direct action or through elected representatives Definition in my own words: a form of government where people in a country vote and elect representatives to govern their country	Characteristics of a democracy: • people set up their own government • leaders are elected • the majority decides • has a written constitution • has free and open elections • people are active in their own government
DEMOCRACY	
Examples **Nonexamples** United States China Canada North Korea France Brazil Argentina India	Drawings or graphics that illustrate the meaning

Additional focus words in this unit, such as *authoritarian, empire, emperor, turbulence, dynasty,* and *succession,* are often more easily taught organically; that is, the students encounter the words in their reading, explore the meaning of these words through close reading in a number of texts and media, hone their knowledge through research, and use the words as they solve problems and give presentations orally and in writing. This "all the way through" model, dealing with vocabulary before (sometimes with a Fast introduction), during, and after reading, is a hallmark of targeted instruction and calls on students to talk in conversational, problem solving, and presentational modes. Let's explore this idea a bit more.

Vocabulary Framing

Students can organize vocabulary by creating semantically meaningful graphics, or frames, supported by textual evidence. These frames, and the instructional process for using them, mine students' prior knowledge and reading comprehension and prompt rich discussion in which students both use and refine their word knowledge. The frame supports students as they talk and write about what they learn.

A frame differs from a work sheet in that it is part of a process that includes teacher guidance before, during, and after reading, a process captured by the mnemonic "AEIOU":

- Activate and Engage: Tap prior knowledge, ask questions.
- Inquiry and Organize: Chart information learned through reading and discussion.
- Use the chart to generate and share ideas and conclusions.

Vocab-o-gram

One type of frame is a *Vocab-o-gram* (Blachowicz 1986; Blachowicz and Fisher 2010), which uses narrative text structure as an organizing principle. In his language arts class, Jesse, a fourth-grade teacher, is presenting a unit on American life in the 1800s. The students are about to read *Keep the Lights Burning, Abbie* (Roop, Roop, and Hanson 1987), which is based on an actual occurrence that took place in 1856. In the book, the keeper of a lighthouse off the coast of Maine entrusts his daughter, Abbie, with the task of keeping the candle-powered lighthouse lights burning while he sails back to the mainland for supplies. A huge storm prevents him from returning for several weeks, and Abbie keeps the lamps burning, getting up several times each night to climb the towers to check them and scraping ice from the windows so the lights can be seen at sea.

To introduce the book, Jesse helps his students focus on the structure and grammar of narrative by having them organize important vocabulary and story elements in a Vocab-o-gram. He also assigns each student two words (chosen based on the student's stage of development and attached to the Vocab-o-gram on small sticky notes) to watch for while reading. He asks students to note the location of each word and use context clues and reference books to determine its meaning. He also encourages them to add to the Vocab-o-gram any other interesting words they encounter. (One student's Vocab-o-gram is shown in Figure 3–11.)

Figure 3–11 A Student's Vocab-o-gram for *Keep the Lights Burning, Abbie*

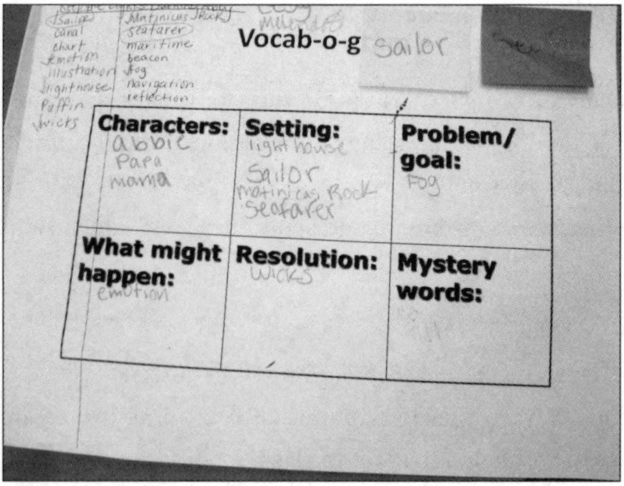

After they have read the book, students use the Vocab-o-gram to help them discuss setting, characters, events, problems, and solutions. They then present their learning to the group. For example, lamp wicks, things with which very few of the students were familiar, are very important to the story. *Wicks* is one of Karima's words, and she tells the class:

Okay, you know that little string in a candle? Well, in these lamps wicks are like pieces of string that go into the oil. You need to keep checking them to make sure they are not all burnt up. If they are, you have to put in a new one. So, a wick is the string that burns in a candle or oil lamp.

After the class discussion, Jesse asks the students to reflect their current thinking on their Vocab-o-gram in a different-color pencil. He determines that additional vocabulary work is unnecessary and, as an extension activity, has them use their Vocab-o-grams to write a summary of the book (again differentiated by the students' level of development: some summarize the entire book, others focus on just an aspect or two, such as the characters and the main event). He encourages them to include words that describe the characters' appearance and behavior, thus further integrating their learning. He assesses these summaries to determine to what extent the students have learned the targeted vocabulary and revisits any words that need clarification.

Frames are often used for some performance activity that involves writing, speaking, media, art, or some combination of several of these. In a recent classroom study using Vocab-o-gram frames, fourth and fifth graders used twice as many targeted vocabulary words in their unprompted summary writing when using frames as did control students reading the same selections. They also used twice as many words compared to their own writing after reading other selections without using a frame to scaffold their learning and writing (Blachowicz, Bates, and Cieply 2013).

Knowledge Ratings

Another type of frame useful for social studies and science topics is Knowledge Rating (Blachowicz and Fisher 2010). Rating students' prior knowledge is a fast way to preview words connected to a topic. It also provides information on students' background knowledge related to the topic. John, an eighth-grade science teacher, is preparing to teach a unit on plant and animal cells. He doesn't want to do much preteaching of vocabulary. He wants students to come to understand the words through their reading and through the activities and experiments. However, he wants the students to have a purpose for their reading. He begins by giving students a list of the eight essential vocabulary words (Figure 3–12). He makes sure that he reads all the words aloud, since some of the words may be in his students' oral vocabulary. He also wants to be sure that his English language learners hear how the words are pronounced. He then asks the students to indicate their familiarity with each word, explaining that he expects this to vary.

Figure 3–12 Science Words for Knowledge Rating

Directions: Here are some words we will be learning in our next science unit. Please place an X in the box that best describes your understanding of this word.				
Word	No clue	Have heard or seen it	Know the word	Know it well and can define it
membrane				
nucleus				
mitochondrion				
ribosome				
cytoplasm				
vacuole				
protoplasm				
organelle				

After the students have filled in the chart independently, he asks them to form groups of four and discuss which words are the most unfamiliar. Each group is asked to report to the class on one of the words they discussed. John listens and does some clarifying, but for the most part he uses the discussion to motivate and engage the students with the topic. By the end of the lesson, John has a clear picture of how he can differentiate his instruction to meet the needs of his students. He follows up by teaching individual words needing more attention. He assigns different words to different teams for the Inquiry and Organize phase and the "all the way through" process continues much as in the Vocab-o-gram example.

Once you have used a framing device or two, you will be able to apply the "AEIOU" process in connection with any number and variety of frames. The sum of group members' knowledge captured in a frame is always greater than that of an individual, and students use the frame to guide the close reading through which they create, support, and share ideas orally and in writing, as called for by the Common Core State Standards (National Governors Association Center for Best Practices and Council of Chief State School Officers 2010a).

Possible Sentences

The Possible-Sentences Strategy (Stahl and Kapinus 1991) expands students' word knowledge by asking them to contextualize words they will encounter in an upcoming unit of instruction. Using their background knowledge, students then connect these words to ideas in the text. This strategy also helps students set a purpose for their reading.

Joan uses possible sentences to introduce a section on erosion to her seventh-grade science class. She begins by activating and engaging, listing nine essential/important vocabulary words (see below). Using eight to twelve words is optimal. This provides students with words that are central to the topic but also provides enough words so that a variety of sentences can be constructed. She makes sure to pronounce all the words and then asks the students to use as many of the words as possible to create sentences that might be part of the section. If necessary for some students, the teacher may provide a very brief definition of one or more words.

erosion	landslides
sediment	mudflow
deposition	slumps
gravity	creep
mass movement	

After the students have created their sentences independently, she has them share in groups of three or four. She then leads a whole-class discussion, asking each group to share one sentence. (She accepts all sentences and doesn't clarify misconceptions.) Joan then writes the sentences on the whiteboard, underlining the vocabulary words, and reminds the students that these are sentences they might expect to find in the text (see these sentences below). Notice how different this activity is from traditional "look up the list" activities, with the teacher offering explanations of the words as needed and students composing and discussing the words and their sentences together.

Erosion moves dirt and rocks.
You can see sediment from erosion.
Deposition is something that is deposited.
Mass movement is caused by erosion.
Gravity keeps us from floating off into space.
Landslides and mudflows contain a lot of dirt.
Dirt slumps and creeps during erosion.

Then, prompting the students to inquire and organize, Joan invites them to verify their predictions by reading the text. She asks them to take notes, especially when they encounter one of the initial vocabulary words.

In the next step, Joan and the students go back and reread the possible sentences on the board. The students locate and cite information in the text that confirms or requires them to adjust their sentences. They place a *C* next to the sentence if it can be confirmed in the text, an *A* if it needs to be adjusted. See below.

C	<u>Erosion</u> moves dirt and rocks.
	Evidence from text: Erosion is a process by which natural forces move rock and soil.
C	You can see <u>sediment</u> from <u>erosion</u>.
	Evidence from text: Erosion moves material called sediment.
A	<u>Deposition</u> is something that is deposited.
	Evidence: Deposition occurs when sediment is deposited by erosion. Deposition changes the shape of the land.
C/A	<u>Mass movement</u> is caused by erosion.
	Evidence from text: Erosion and deposition both take place during mass movement.

Teaching Word-Learning Strategies

As we noted in Section 2, students can be taught to infer the meanings of unknown or partially known words by using context clues and analyzing root words, prefixes and suffixes, and Latin and Greek word roots.

Using Context

When stuck on a new word, students can use external context and internal context (word parts) to help. The building of declarative knowledge about types of context is one of the most developed parts of traditional word study curricula, and we won't duplicate it here. What is important is including procedural learning. Baumann and colleagues (2002) formulated "The Vocabulary Rule" (see Figure 3–13), which stresses the need for students to learn to use context and word parts in a process-oriented way.

Figure 3–13   The Vocabulary Rule

> ## The Vocabulary Rule
>
> When you come to a word and don't know what it means:
>
> 1. Try to SAY IT OUT LOUD. It may be part of your oral vocabulary.
>
> 2. Look for CONTEXT CLUES. Read the sentences around the word to see whether there are hints to its meaning.
>
> 3. Look for WORD PART CLUES. See if you can break the word into a root word and prefixes and suffixes to help figure out its meaning. Look also for word parts like -vis or -vid ("to see") to help you decide what it means.
>
> 4. Think of a WORD IN ANOTHER LANGUAGE (Spanish, for example) that looks like or sounds like the English word [in schools with diverse languages].
>
> 5. Try ANOTHER STRATEGY, such as reading on, asking someone, or using a dictionary or thesaurus.

Process lessons for context clues would include teaching the major types of context clues (i.e., definition, synonym, antonym, example, apposition, global context) and then giving students plenty of practice in real contexts. Ask students to locate the unknown word and look around (before or after) the word for the types of clues presented. Students can also look within the word (internal context) for word parts that help them understand the word. What is important is that students find the evidence for their conclusion about the word and then end up by asking, "Does this make sense?"

Using Word Parts

One of the best ways we have found to emphasize word parts is to keep a yearlong chart of word part families (Baumann, Ware, and Edwards 2002). Figure 3–14 shows an example of word part families that are organized into meaningful sets. The chart shows prefixes for the "not" family with examples from a Spanish/English two-way immersion class.

Figure 3–14 Prefix Chart for the Not or Opposite Family

Prefix Families: The NOT or OPPOSITE Family			
Family	**Prefix**	**Examples**	**meanings**
"Not" Prefix Family	**dis-**	**dis**honest, **dis**respectful	**not** honest, **not** respectful
	un-	**un**chained, **un**happy	**not** chained, **not** happy
	in-	**in**correct, **in**visible,	**not** correct, **not** visible,
	im-	**im**possible, **im**practical	**not** possible, **not** practical
	non-	**non**fiction, **non**living	**not** fiction, **not** living

In another process for learning word parts, Josie, a fifth-grade teacher, used morphology boxes (Ogle 2011). These are boxes that represent the number of meaningful parts of a word (see below). When students tried to analyze the word *profitable*, rather than dividing it into syllables (which led them to believe it was something about how *pro* athletic shoes *fit* people), Josie placed two boxes on the board and asked them to place two parts of the word in appropriate places:

profit	able

The students filled the first one with *profit* and the second with *able*, which led them to a more appropriate meaning for *profitable* in the text sentence "Their business was a profitable one." This helped them develop a strategy of looking for the larger meaningful parts for determining word meaning and then checking with the context. Keep in mind that the number of boxes is dependent upon the number of meaningful word parts. If the word had been *unprofitable,* Josie would have used three boxes.

Using References

When all else fails, the Vocabulary Rule directs students to a reference or a more knowledgeable person. Students come to the dictionary having examined an unknown word in text so that they can use the dictionary sensibly. One way to encourage student dictionary use participation is to appoint a "dictionary director" each day. Whenever a word, the meaning of which is unclear, surfaces in class discussion, the dictionary director looks it up on a dictionary website (the computer screen can be projected on a SMART Board). Dictionary.com (www.dictionary.reference.com) and the Longman Dictionary of Contemporary English (www.ldoceonline.com) are two excellent sites (the Longman site defines words in more ordinary language). Longman also publishes excellent dictionaries of idioms.

"And Now for Something Completely Different": Engaging Review

Something that crosses all the components of a comprehensive approach is keeping words visible and involving students in engaging and pleasurable review. In our summative qualitative research on our four years of work with teachers and students (Blachowicz, Bates, and Cieply 2013) and in our coaching development work (Blachowicz and Cobb 2007), one aspect of our process that was singled out by both teachers and students as valuable and important was recording and review.

Semantic Word Walls

Keeping words visible in the classroom makes a vital contribution to developing both word knowledge and word consciousness. That's why we see so many words walls as we visit classrooms around the country. But *having* a word wall and *using* a word wall can be entirely different things (Harmon et al. 2009).

We discussed the various research bases for repetition and word choice in Section 2. MCVIP teachers review between eight and fourteen word wall words a week as "everybody words"—all students are responsible for being able to use them in writing and discussion. Though there was some grumbling when this policy was introduced, both teachers and students now agree that this ritual is important to their word consciousness. Most teachers use some form of tally board, either with or without a point system, as a means for students to report instances of seeing, hearing, or using the week's focus words.

Be a Mind Reader

To review words, you can choose from among a number of quick and playful activities (Be a Mind Reader, Connect Two, Hot Seat, and others). Be a Mind Reader (Cunningham 2008) is a favorite. It takes about five minutes to prepare and five minutes to carry out in the classroom. Choose a "mystery" word from among the weekly vocabulary words and prepare a set of five clues that, by process of elimination, will reveal the word. Have students number their papers from 1 to 5. Read each clue, writing or displaying it as you do so. Students write a word from the list that fits each clue and the preceding clues. When the fifth clue is revealed, all students should be able to solve the "mystery" word.

The weekly word review chart in Kelly's third-grade classroom displays these words:

tissue	reveal	assembly	committee
exchange	assume	static	enthusiasm
council	defeated	identify	effect

She asks students to take out their whiteboards and number from 1 to 5 (see Figure 3–15).

Figure 3–15   Be a Mind Reader Whiteboard

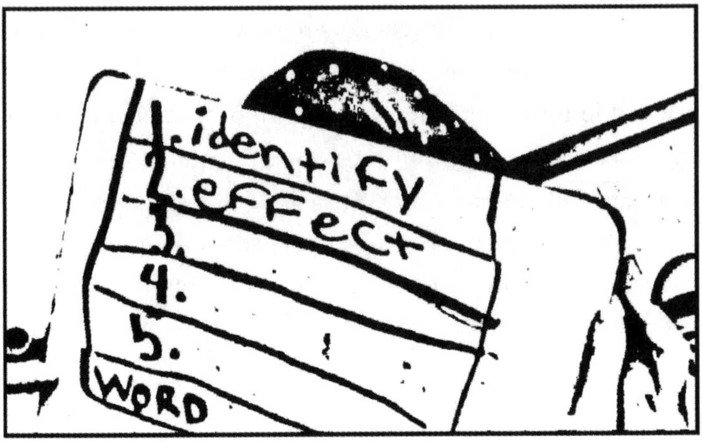

Then they listen to Kelly's five clues in an attempt to determine the mystery word Kelly is thinking of:

Clue 1: [this should always be the first clue]: "It's a word on our chart."

Clue 2: "It's a noun."

Clue 3: "It has more than two syllables."

Clue 4: "It's related to the word *energy*."

Clue 5: "If you back our team, the Thunderbirds, you have plenty of this."

[Answer: *enthusiasm*]

Games like this allow students to review the week's words, their features and definitions, in a playful way. The clues often contain significant metalinguistic terms (*syllable, vowel, prefix, root word, synonym, antonym*), thus giving students another opportunity to review and use these words. After students are familiar with the process, student teams can be challenged to create the mind-reader clues and lead the activity. (Students love this and other word games, so always prepare three or four for the weekly review or those other 3 × 5 moments!)

Students became so attuned to the words that they often blurt out, "That's one of our words," when they came across them during class or even on standardized tests. To encourage this kind of paying attention while minimizing interruptions, you can ask students to use the *V* (for vocabulary) hand sign more commonly known as "V for victory," whenever they notice a word they've studied.

Our classroom observations prove that word consciousness is flowering. Several teachers have told us that their students remind them that Friday is almost over and they haven't yet had their vocabulary review. One teacher being so reminded turned around to find the weekly chart and, turning back, discovered students lined up, word-bearing sticky notes in hand, ready to talk about the words they had seen, heard, and used that week. Weekly review usually turns out to be a surprising hit with teachers and students alike and a great help in making students word-conscious learners.

Being Accountable

As we related in Section 1, vocabulary assessment is an ongoing issue for teachers. However, we believe that vocabulary assessment must be situated within the larger picture of accountability. Figure 3–16 is a graphic representation of the three interactive components of accountability that we feel are essential for building an effective program of vocabulary instruction. The three components include evidence-based instructional practice, differentiated instruction, and both formative and summative assessments.

Components of Accountability

Providing instruction that is grounded in evidence and best practice ensures that you take responsibility for your teaching and for students' learning. Differentiating your instruction allows you to meet the needs of all students, including English language learners and at-risk

Figure 3–16 The Three Components of Accountability

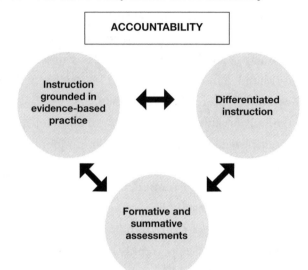

students. Establishing formative and summative measures that accurately show student growth in vocabulary knowledge lets you share this growth with both students and parents. It's important to remember that these components are flexible and interactive. Each component relies on the others to create a system of instruction that meets the needs of all students.

Defining the Role of Assessment

Assessment is one component of accountability. Fundamentally, assessment provides information you need to help students. Formative assessment is sometimes viewed as assessment for learning. Regular and engaging review, as used by teachers in the MCVIP study to ensure student accountability (see Section 2), is a type of formative assessment. Students are able to "show what they know" through writing and oral presentations. The teachers can then use this information to determine the next steps for instruction or plan for additional small-group instruction.

Summative assessment is sometimes referred to as "assessment of learning." Summative assessment is used at the conclusion of a unit to determine whether your students have reached the expected levels of proficiency. It can be used in connection with grading and reporting. Rubrics assessing personal word books or content dictionaries provide an example of meaningful summative assessment that can be used for reporting purposes.

For background on why assessment is important

see Section 2, page 40

Assessments must be useful for both you and your students. Students need to understand the expectations for learning as well as the criteria you will use to judge successful achievement. Assessment should not be a guessing game you and your students play. Assessment should also be followed by feedback and corrective instruction. Later in this section we will share examples of both formative and summative assessments of vocabulary knowledge. In every case, assessment, whether it is formative or summative, should not mark the end of learning but rather be a checkpoint for the level of learning as well as a guide to what needs to happen next.

Evaluating Your System of Accountability

In Section 2, Camille provided a wealth of information on instruction that is grounded in research and best practice. Earlier in this section, we provided strategies that allow for differentiation. The Flood, Fast, Focus framework supports highly effective vocabulary instruction. Implementing it requires planning and commitment, along with accountability. Planning ensures that your work is both intentional and purposeful. Commitment enables you to honor your pledge to effect change. Accountability provides the data you need to monitor, measure, and make informed decisions regarding your instruction and your students' learning. As you begin planning and make the commitment to change, consider these questions to provide data for accountability.

- What research and evidence am I using to ground my instruction?
- How do I use instructional strategies to differentiate instruction?
- Is both formative and summative assessment part of my instructional planning?

While it is certainly possible to develop a plan on your own, doing so with one or more "critical friends" has many benefits. Dialogues with other educators about teaching and learning vocabulary stimulate professional growth. Grappling with issues related to selecting words, promoting student independence, finding time for vocabulary instruction in the classroom day, and assessing student learning are less daunting when colleagues share their knowledge and expertise. Using the checklist in Figure 3–2 to rate your school's vocabulary environment is the first step in the planning process.

Deciding on which words to teach, determining available resources, and establishing schedules for vocabulary instruction can also be a collaborative effort. A planning grid like the one in Figure 3–17 will help you get ready by specifying the words you have selected and the methods of instruction you have chosen.

As you begin to implement the framework, collaborative celebrations of successes and responses to challenges can help you keep on track. Working in a supportive environment strengthens your commitment to continue. Hearing about what works in other classrooms gives you ideas to incorporate into your own instruction. Sharing struggles and frustrations with colleagues creates a support system that helps you examine and improve your practice. Now let's move on to some strategies for formative and summative vocabulary assessments.

Assessment Strategies

Teacher-constructed, criterion-referenced assessments (Bean and Swan Dagen 2006) are an alternative to standardized vocabulary tests. These criterion-referenced assessments include a variety of formats—

Figure 3–17 Planning Grid for Word Selection and Instruction

CHOOSING WORDS and PLANNING INSTRUCTION—FAST, FOCUS, FLOOD

Unit Name _____ Topic/Big Idea _____

STUDENT STRATEGY words: words students will figure out using the context or with other strategies; teacher scaffolding as needed	ESSENTIAL FOR UNDERSTANDING	NICE TO KNOW
FAST words: *key vocabulary that the teacher teaches using Fast synonym, Teaching Individual Words (TIW) model, or other brief instruction*		
FOCUS words: *key vocabulary for which teacher uses an "AEIOU" "all the way through" method with vocabulary frame to support students*		
FLOOD words: *additional vocabulary for word wall, wordplay, building relational sets*		

multiple-choice items, cloze procedures, requests for target words in a constructed response. Below are some examples in the context of a unit on the westward movement:

- Multiple-Choice Item

  Manifest Destiny was about [choose the best answer]:

  A. Abolishing slavery

  B. Expanding territories

  C. Maintaining freedom of religion

  D. Choosing a new form of government

- Cloze Procedure

  In 1803, the United States acquired a large portion of land from _____. This was called the _____ and included land that was west of the _____ River.

- Constructed Response

  The area between the Mississippi River and the Pacific Ocean was explored by _____.

Students can also identify words on the basis of their parts or define word parts based on a series of provided words.

The type of assessment used depends on the purpose. What type of information are you trying to gather about student learning? As Camille mentioned in Section 2, a multiple-choice objective test provides a fairly low-level assessment of vocabulary. Using a cloze or constructed response assessment adds some context, but still does not provide an opportunity to assess depth of word knowledge. These types of criterion-referenced assessments can be used. However, there are other ways to think about vocabulary assessment.

Student Writing. Student writing is rich source material for formatively assessing students' knowledge of vocabulary. Response journals, quick-writes, and extended responses to reading can all inform your vocabulary instruction. Questions and prompts that lead students to reflect on and include selected vocabulary in their written responses make them conscious of words. They begin to understand that words are not meant to be learned one time, for one unit or subject, but rather that words are gateways to expressing ideas and helping them become better readers and writers. Here are two sample prompts for written responses:

- Response journal. From your vocabulary journal this week, select a word that you have used at least once outside the classroom. Explain the situation and why you selected this word to use.
- Quick-write. What is the relationship between acute and obtuse angles? Explain the features of each in your response.

Presentations. Student presentations in both language arts and content areas should be assessed in terms of how well students use vocabulary to present information. The Common Core speaking and listening standards include comprehension and collaboration as well as presentation and knowledge of ideas. Oral presentations should be assessed using rubrics (as mentioned earlier) that include features of both delivery and content. You should always share these rubrics with students in advance so they are aware of the expectations. Including student use of vocabulary in the rubric gives students another way to show their level of growth in word learning.

Discussion. You can also assess vocabulary while observing small-group and whole-class discussions. Anecdotal records of students' use of academic vocabulary in posing and responding to questions, stating ideas, and summarizing provide valuable information. For example, because Lupe wants to check how and when her students use academic vocabulary during discussions in her fourth-grade geometry unit, she uses an observation form to record student responses, selecting only the words she feels are essential (see Figure 3–18).

Figure 3–18 Math Vocabulary Used in Class Discussions
During a Geometry Unit

	Ann	Jorge	Paul	Kim	Maya	Cole
segments	P R	R		P R		
lines	R			P R S	P R S	
angles	R S	P R S	R	P R S	P R	
parallel	R S			P R		P R S
rays	R	P R			P R	R
perpendicular	P		P R			P R

P = posing questions

R = responding to questions

S = stating ideas/summarizing

Content Assessment. You can also integrate vocabulary assessment with content assessment. If you have introduced students to the reading strategy of analyzing character traits, you might say, "Think about the words we've been using to describe character traits in our literature circle books. We've talked about characters who are ingenious, selfless, and ambitious, among other traits. I would like you to think about some of the people we've been learning about in social studies as we've studied the westward movement. Select two people and describe their character traits. Be sure to provide evidence for your thinking by citing examples from our social studies text." This type of writing aligns with the expectations of the Common Core State Standards (CCSS.ELA-Literacy.RL.5.3/CCSS.ELA-Literacy.RI.5.3).

Some vocabulary strategies lend themselves to both formative and summative assessments. In the earlier example, Lupe uses Fast teaching of word sorts as a formative assessment. As students group and categorize words, she notes student understanding and uses this information to guide and drive further instruction. These word sorts are not graded. At the completion of the geometry unit, Lupe asks her students to sort the words again (see Figure 3–19). This time she provides categories based on what she expects them to have learned and asks them to explain their thinking in writing—to demonstrate their understanding of the concepts taught within the unit. This is a summative assessment that can be graded.

Figure 3–19 Word Sort Used as a Summative Assessment

Directions: Sort these words according to the headings listed below the words. After sorting the words, write a paragraph for each heading explaining why you included those words.

rhombus	*obtuse*	*rays*
rectangle	*parallel*	*quadrilateral*
acute	*right*	*perpendicular*
segments	*square*	

Two-Dimensional Figures	Angles	Lines

The knowledge-rating chart John uses in his science class is another example of formative assessment. It allows John to measure his students' knowledge of specific content words. John doesn't grade the knowledge rating but uses the data to group students and plan instructional activities. At the conclusion of the unit, rather than give students a multiple-choice or matching vocabulary test, John uses another knowledge-rating chart as a summative assessment (Figure 3–20). Students demonstrate their learning by defining, contextualizing, or illustrating their understanding of the essential vocabulary.

Figure 3–20   Knowledge-Rating Chart Used as a Summative Assessment

Directions: Here are words we've been learning in our science unit. For each word, explain what you know. This can include a definition, an example, and/or a diagram with labels.

Word	What I know about this word
membrane	
nucleus	
mitochondrion	
ribosome	
cytoplasm	
vacuole	
protoplasm	
organelle	

Next Steps

One must be drenched in words, literally soaked in them, to have the right ones form themselves into the proper pattern at the right moment.

— Hart Crane, American poet (1899–1932)

Part of the joy of teaching comes from an awareness of how much there is to learn and how worthwhile the learning is. Just as word learning is incremental, so is learning about vocabulary instruction. Word learners need repeated and varied exposures to a word. Teachers need repeated and varied exposure to research, best practice strategies, and fellow practitioners. This deepens our knowledge and moves our practice from novice to expert. Wherever you are on your journey, we hope that you will consider the research and strategies we've shared with you. We encourage you to take the next step. We hope that you will invite someone else to come along with you!

AFTERWORD

NELL K. DUKE

Few people reading this book have not, at some point in their school careers, been given a list of words to look up in the dictionary and use in a sentence. Many have assigned this task themselves. Charlene Cobb and Camille Blachowicz give us a wealth of alternatives to this age-old instructional practice. They help us understand that these alternative practices are likely to work much better, and why.

One of the things I appreciate most about this book is that the authors focus not only on raising vocabulary knowledge and achievement, but on raising something more elusive, but perhaps no less important—a genuine interest in words. This interest is unlikely to derive from an assigned vocabulary list tackled with the dictionary, and much more likely to derive from such activities as thinking about how to represent a word visually, as in word square (p. 48), playing games with words, as in Be a Mind Reader (p. 69), or talking with friends about interesting words encountered in a text, as in Vocab-o-gram (p. 59). An interest in words increases awareness, attention, and engagement, which in turn is likely to foster word learning and achievement.

When students are interested in words, it is likely to make our work as educators more enjoyable. Recall from Section 2, Figure 2–1: "What's Happening in Students' Heads While They're Looking Up the List?"

Hmm, the word is GLIPPLE. *Let's see.* . . . [finding it in the dictionary] *OK,* GLIPPLE . . . *hmm, let's look* . . . *I see* GLIPPLE, *OK* . . . *I know I should write the first definition but that will take me forever. Here's the shortest definition. I'll write that. OK, definition done.*

Now a sentence. OK, it's a verb. How about, "I decided to GLIPPLE." No, she'll catch on if I do that and just have it the last word. How about "I GLIPPLED yesterday." Yeah, that's it. Done.

You no more want to read the fruits of this process than students want to engage in it. The alternative practices Cobb and Blachowicz describe are more interesting for you, too. I myself encountered a new term in this book—*Tom Swifty*—a phrase that includes a kind of joke or play on words (a pun) as in *"I need to sharpen my pencil," said Anne bluntly.* My delight in learning this new term reminded me of the delight in words we want to foster in students. Thus I end with this: It's time to give up "Look up the list" in favor of the many more engaging and effective vocabulary practices available, and I mean that definitively.

REFERENCES

Au, K. H. 1997. "Ownership, Literacy Achievement, and Students of Diverse Cultural Backgrounds." In *Reading Engagement: Motivating Readers Through Integrated Instruction*, ed. J. T. Guthrie and A. Wigfield, 168–82. Newark, DE: International Reading Association.

Baumann, J. F. 2009. "Intensity in Vocabulary Instruction and Effects on Reading Comprehension." *Topics in Language Disorders* 29: 312–28.

Baumann, J. F., C. L. Z. Blachowicz, P. C. Manyak, M. F. Graves, and S. Olejnik. 2009–2012. *Development of a Multi-Faceted, Comprehensive, Vocabulary Instructional Program for the Upper-Elementary Grades* [R305A090163]. Washington, DC: U.S. Department of Education, Institute of Education Sciences, National Center for Education Research (Reading and Writing Program).

Baumann, J. F., E. C. Edwards, E. Boland, S. Olejnik, and E. W. Kame'enui. 2003. "Vocabulary Tricks: Effects of Instruction in Morphology and Context on Fifth-Grade Students' Ability to Derive and Infer Word Meanings." *American Educational Research Journal* 40: 447–94.

Baumann, J. F., E. C. Edwards, G. Font, C. A. Tereshinski, E. J. Kame'enui, and S. Olejnik. 2002. "Teaching Morphemic and Contextual Analysis to Fifth-Grade Students." *Reading Research Quarterly* 37: 150–76.

Baumann, J. F., and M. F. Graves. 2010. "What Is Academic Vocabulary?" *Journal of Adolescent & Adult Literacy* 54: 4–12.

Baumann, J. F., P. C. Manyak, H. Peterson, C. L. Z. Blachowicz, C. Cieply, A. Bates, J. Davis, J. Arner, M. Graves, and S. Templeton. 2011. "Windows on Formative/Design-Based Research on Vocabulary Instruction: Findings and Methodological Challenges." Symposium at the annual meeting of the Literacy Research Association, Jacksonville, FL, December 2.

Baumann, J. F., D. Ware, and E. C. Edwards. 2007. "'Bumping into Spicy, Tasty Words That Catch Your Tongue': A Formative Experiment on Vocabulary Instruction." *The Reading Teacher* 62: 108–22.

Bean, R. M., and A. Swan Dagen. 2006. "Vocabulary Assessment: A Key to Planning Vocabulary Instruction." In *Vocabulary-Enriched Classroom: Practices for Improving the Reading Performance of All Students in Grades 3 and Up*, ed. J. Mangieri and C. Collins Block. New York: Scholastic.

Beck, I. L., and M. G. McKeown. 1991. "Conditions of Vocabulary Acquisition." In *Handbook of Reading Research: Volume II*, ed. R. Barr, M. Kamil, P. Mosenthal, and P. D. Pearson, 789–814. New York: Longman.

———. 2007. "Increasing Young Low-Income Children's Oral Vocabulary Repertoires Through Rich and Focused Instruction." *Elementary School Journal* 107: 251–71.

Beck, I. L., M. G. McKeown, and L. Kucan. 2008. *Creating Robust Vocabulary: Frequently Asked Questions & Extended Examples*. New York: Guilford.

Beck, I. L., C. A. Perfetti, and M. G. McKeown. 1982. "The Effects of Long-Term Vocabulary Instruction on Lexical Access and Reading Comprehension." *Journal of Educational Psychology* 74: 506–21.

Becker, W. C. 1977. "Teaching Reading and Language to the Disadvantaged—What We Have Learned from Field Research." *Harvard Educational Review* 47: 518–43.

Bergelson, E., and D. Swingley. 2013. "The Acquisition of Abstract Words by Young Infants." *Cognition* 127: 391–97.

Biemiller, A. 2005. "Size and Sequence in Vocabulary Development: Implications for Choosing Words for Primary Grade Vocabulary Instruction." In *Teaching and Learning Vocabulary: Bringing Research to Practice*, ed. E. H. Hiebert and M. Kamil, 223–42. Mahwah, NJ: Erlbaum.

Biemiller, A., and C. Boote. 2006. "An Effective Method for Building Meaning Vocabulary in Primary Grades." *Journal of Educational Psychology* 98: 44–62.

Biemiller, A., and N. Slonim. 2001. "Estimating Root Word Vocabulary Growth in Normative and Advantaged Populations: Evidence for a Common Sequence of Vocabulary Acquisition." *Journal of Educational Psychology* 93: 498–520.

Blachowicz, C. L. Z. 1986. "Making Connections: Alternatives to Vocabulary Notebook." *Journal of Reading* 29: 643–49.

Blachowicz, C. L. Z., A. Bates, and C. Cieply. 2012a. "Teacher Perceptions and Contributions in a Formative Long-Term Vocabulary Intervention." Annual conference of the American Educational Research Association, Vancouver, BC, April 16.

———. 2012b. "Vocabulary Framing: Supporting Student Vocabulary Learning and Language Use in a Multifaceted Vocabulary Instruction Project." Annual conference of the International Reading Association, Chicago, IL, April 30.

———. 2013. "Teachers Meet (and Exceed!) the Vocabulary Challenges of the Common Core State Standards: Celebrating Teacher Tested Strategies." Paper presented at annual conference of the International Reading Association, San Antonio, TX, April 20.

Blachowicz, C. L. Z., and J. A. Baumann. 2012. "Vocabulary Standards for Grades 3–5: Connecting the Common Core State Standards to Evidence-Based Instruction." In *Connecting Literacy Instruction to the Common Core School Standards*, ed. L. M. Morrow, T. Shanahan, and K. K. Wixson. New York: Guilford.

Blachowicz, C., and C. Cobb. 2007. *Action Tools: Vocabulary in the Content Areas.* Alexandria, VA: ASCD.

Blachowicz, C. L. Z., and P. Fisher. 2010. *Teaching Vocabulary in All Classrooms*, 4th ed. Englewood Cliffs, NJ: Merrill/Prentice Hall.

———. 2012. "Putting the 'Fun' Back in Fundamental." In *Vocabulary Instruction: Research to Practice*, 2d ed., ed. E. Kame'enui and J. Baumann. New York: Guilford.

Blachowicz, C. L. Z., P. J. L. Fisher, D. Ogle, and S. Watts-Taffe. 2006. "Vocabulary: Questions from the Classroom." *Reading Research Quarterly* 41: 524–39.

———. 2013. *Teaching Academic Vocabulary K–8: Effective Practices Across the Curriculum.* New York: Guilford.

Blachowicz, C. L. Z., and C. Obrochta. 2005. "Vocabulary Visits: Developing Content Vocabulary in the Primary Grades." *Reading Teacher* 59: 262–69.

———. 2007. "'Tweaking Practice': Modifying Read-Alouds to Enhance Content Vocabulary Learning in Grade 1." *National Reading Conference Yearbook,* 111–21. Oak Creek, WI: National Reading Conference.

Bos, C. S., and P. L. Anders. 1990. "Effects of Interactive Vocabulary Instruction on the Vocabulary Learning and Reading Comprehension of Junior-High Learning Disabled Students." *Learning Disability Quarterly* 13: 31–42.

———. 1992. "Using Interactive Teaching and Learning Strategies to Promote Text Comprehension and Content Learning for Students with Learning Disabilities." *International Journal of Disability, Development and Education* 39: 225–38.

Bowers, P. N., J. R. Kirby, and S. H. Deacon. 2010. "The Effects of Morphological Instruction on Literacy Skills: A Systematic Review of the Literature." *Review of Educational Research* 80: 144–79.

Britton, J. N. 1987. Writing and Reading in the Classroom. Center for the Study of Writing Technical Report #8. Berkeley, CA: Center for the Study of Writing, University of California, Berkeley; Pittsburgh, PA: Carnegie Mellon University.

Campbell, J. R., K. Voelkl, and P. L. Donahue. 1997. *NAEP 1996 Trends in Academic Progress.* NCES Publication No. 97–985. Washington, DC: U.S. Department of Education.

Carlisle, J. F., C. McBride-Chang, W. Nagy, and T. Nunes. 2010. "Effects of Instruction in Morphological Awareness on Literacy

Achievement: An Integrative Review." *Reading Research Quarterly* 45 (4): 464–87.

Carlo, M. S., D. August, and C. E. Snow. 2005. "Sustained Vocabulary-Learning Strategies for English Language Learners." In *Teaching and Learning Vocabulary: Bringing Research to Practice*, ed. E. H. Hiebert and M. Kamil, 137–53. Mahwah, NJ: Erlbaum.

Cervetti, G. N., P. D. Pearson, J. Barber, E. H. Hiebert, and M. A. Bravo. 2007. "Integrating Literacy and Science: The Research We Have, the Research We Need." In Shaping Literacy Achievement, ed. M. Pressley, A. K. Billman, K. Perry, K. Refitt, and J. Reynolds, 157–74. New York: Guilford.

Cunningham, A. E. 2005. "Vocabulary Growth Through Independent Reading and Reading Aloud to Children." In *Teaching and Learning Vocabulary: Bringing Research to Practice*, ed. E. H. Hiebert and M. L. Kamil, 45–68. Mahwah, NJ: Erlbaum.

Cunningham, P. M. 2008. *Phonics They Use: Words for Reading and Writing*. New York: Pearson.

Dale, E., and J. P. O'Rourke. 1976. *The Living Word Vocabulary*. Chicago: Field Enterprises.

D'Anna, C. A., E. B. Zechmeister, and J. W. Hall. 1991. "Toward a Meaningful Definition of Vocabulary Size." *Journal of Reading Behavior* 23 (1): 109–22.

Davis, F. B. 1944. "Fundamental Factors of Comprehension in Reading." *Psychometrika* 9: 185–97.

———. 1968. "Research in Comprehension in Reading." *Reading Research Quarterly* 3: 499–545.

Durso, F. T., and K. A. Coggins. 1991. "Organized Instruction for the Improvement of Word Knowledge Skills." *Journal of Educational Psychology* 83: 108–12.

Elleman, A. M., J. Lindo Endia, P. Morphy, and D. L. Compton. 2009. "The Impact of Vocabulary Instruction on Passage-Level

Comprehension of School-Age Children: A Meta-Analysis." *Journal of Research on Educational Effectiveness* 2: 1–44.

Eller, G., C. C. Pappas, and E. Brown. 1988. "The Lexical Development of Kindergartners: Learning from Written Context." *Journal of Reading Behavior* 20: 5–24.

Evans, K. 2002. "Fifth-Grade Students' Perceptions of How They Experience Literature Discussion Groups." *Reading Research Quarterly* (January–February): 46–49.

Fisher, P. J. L., C. L. Z. Blachowicz, and J. C. Smith. 1991. "Vocabulary Learning in Literature Discussion Groups." In *Learner Factors/Teacher Factors: Issues in Literacy Research and Instruction*, ed. J. Zutell and S. McCormick, 201–209. *Fortieth Yearbook of the National Reading Conference*. Chicago: National Reading Conference.

Fisher, P. J., C. L. Z. Blachowicz, and S. Watts-Taffe. 2011. "Vocabulary Instruction: Three Contemporary Issues." In *Handbook of Research on Teaching the English Language Arts*, 3d ed., ed. D. Lapp and D. Fisher, 252–57. New York: Routledge.

Frayer, D. A., W. C. Frederick, and H. J. Klausmeier. 1969. "A Schema for Testing the Level of Concept Mastery" (working paper no. 16). Madison, WI: University of Wisconsin.

Fry, E., and T. Rasinski. 2007. *Increasing Fluency with High Frequency Word Phrases*. Huntington Beach, CA: Shell Education.

García, G. E., G. McKoon, and D. August. 2006. "Language and Literacy Assessment of Language-Minority Students." In *Developing Literacy in Second-Language Learners: Report of the National Literacy Panel on Language-Minority Children and Youth*, ed. D. August and T. Shanahan, 597–630. Mahwah, NJ: Erlbaum.

Goodwin, A. P., and S. Ahn. 2010. "A Meta-Analysis of Morphological Interventions: Effects on Literacy Achievement of Children with Literacy Difficulties." *Annals of Dyslexia* 60: 183–208.

Graves, M. F. 1986. "Vocabulary Learning and Instruction." In *Review of Research in Education*, vol. 13, ed. E. Z. Rothkopf, 49–89.

Washington, DC: American Educational Research Association (AERA).

————. 2006. *The Vocabulary Book: Learning and Instruction.* New York: Teachers College Press.

————. 2009. *Teaching Individual Words: One Size Does Not Fit All.* New York: Teachers College Press.

Graves, M. F., and S. M. Watts-Taffe. 2002. "The Place of Word Consciousness in a Research-Based Vocabulary Program." In *What Research Has to Say About Reading Instruction* (3rd ed.), eds. S. J. Samuels and A. E. Farstrup, 140–65. Newark, DE: International Reading Association.

Guthrie, J. T., A. Wigfield, N. M. Humenick, K. C. Perencevich, A. Taboada, and P. Barbosa. 2006. "Influences of Stimulating Tasks on Reading Motivation and Comprehension." *Journal of Educational Research* 99: 232–45.

Haggard, M. R. 1982. "The Vocabulary Self-Selection Strategy: An Active Approach to Word Learning." *Journal of Reading* 26: 634–42.

Harmon, J. M., K. D. Wood, W. B. Hedrick, J. Vintinner, and T. Willeford. 2009. "Interactive Word Walls: More Than Just Reading the Writing on the Walls." Journal of Adolescent & Adult Literacy 52 (5): 398–408.

Hart, B., and T. R. Risley. 1995. *Meaningful Differences in the Everyday Experience of Young American Children.* Baltimore: Brookes.

Hiebert, E. H. 2013. The Text Project. http://textproject.org/. Retrieved July 7, 2013.

Hiebert, E. H., and G. N. Cervetti. 2009. "What Differences in Narrative and Informational Texts Mean for the Learning and Instruction of Vocabulary." In *Vocabulary Instruction: Research to Practice*, 2d ed., ed. E. Kame'enui and J. F. Baumann. New York: Guilford.

Hiebert, E. H., and M. L. Kamil, eds. 2005. *Teaching and Learning Vocabulary: Bringing Research to Practice.* Mahwah, NJ: Erlbaum.

Jiminez, R. J. 1997. "The Strategic Reading Abilities and Potential of Five Low-Literacy Latina/o Readers in Middle School." *Reading Research Quarterly* 32: 224–43.

Johnson, C. J., and J. M. Anglin. 1995. "Qualitative Developments in the Content and Form of Children's Definitions." *Journal of Speech and Hearing Research* 38: 612–29.

Johnston, P. 2004. *Choice Words*. Portland, ME: Stenhouse.

Kame'enui, E., and J. Baumann. 2012. *Vocabulary Instruction: Research to Practice*, 2d ed. New York: Guilford.

Kame'enui, E. J., D. W. Carnine, and R. Freschi. 1982. "Effects of Text Construction and Instructional Procedures for Teaching Word Meanings on Comprehension and Recall." *Reading Research Quarterly* 17: 367–88.

Kim, J. S., and T. G. White. 2008. "Scaffolding Voluntary Summer Reading for Children in Grades 3 to 5: An Experimental Study." *Scientific Studies of Reading* 12: 1–23.

Lubliner, S., and L. Smetana. 2005. "The Effects of Comprehensive Vocabulary Instruction on Title I Students' Metacognitive Word-Learning Skills and Reading Comprehension." *Journal of Literacy Research* 37: 163–99.

Manyak, P. 2007. "Character Trait Vocabulary: A Schoolwide Approach." *The Reading Teacher* 60 (March): 574–77.

Marulis, L. M., and S. B. Neuman. 2010. "The Effects of Vocabulary Intervention on Young Children's Word Learning." *Review of Educational Research* 80 (3): 300–35.

Marzano, R. J., and D. J. Pickering. 2005. *Building Academic Vocabulary Teacher's Manual*. Alexandria, VA: Association for Supervision and Curriculum Development (ASCD).

Matvey, G., J. Dunlosky, and B. L. Schwartz. 2006. "The Effects of Categorical Relatedness on Judgments of Learning (JOLs)." *Memory* 14 (2): 253–61.

McKeown, M. G. 1985. "The Acquisition of Word Meaning from Context by Children of High and Low Ability." *Reading Research Quarterly* 20: 482–96.

———. 1993. "Creating Effective Definitions for Young Word Learners." *Reading Research Quarterly* 28: 16–31.

McKeown, M. G., and I. L. Beck. 1988. "Learning Vocabulary: Different Ways for Different Goals." *Remedial and Special Education* 9: 42–45.

Medina, T. N., J. Snedeker, J. C. Trueswell, and L. R. Gleitman. 2011. "How Words Can and Cannot Be Learned by Observation." Proceedings of the National Academy of Sciences 108: 9014–9019.

Mezynski, K. 1983. "Issues Concerning the Acquisition of Knowledge: Effects of Vocabulary Training on Reading Comprehension." *Review of Educational Research* 53: 253–79.

Nagy, W. E., and P. A. Herman. 1987. "Depth and Breadth of Vocabulary Knowledge: Implications for Acquisition and Instruction." In *The Nature of Vocabulary Acquisition*, ed. M. G. McKeown & M. E. Curtis, 19–35. Hillsdale, NJ: Erlbaum.

Nagy, W. E., P. A. Herman, and R. C. Anderson. 1985. "Learning Words from Context." *Reading Research Quarterly* 20: 233–53.

Nagy, W. E., and J. A. Scott. 2000. "Vocabulary Processes." In *Handbook of Reading Research: Volume III*, ed. M. L. Kamil, P. B. Mosenthal, P. D. Pearson, and R. Barr, 269–84. Mahwah, NJ: Erlbaum.

Nation, I. S. P. 2001. *Learning Vocabulary in Another Language.* Cambridge, UK: Cambridge University Press.

National Governors Association Center for Best Practices and Council of Chief State School Officers. 2010a. *Common Core State Standards.* Washington, DC: National Governors Association Center for Best Practices and Council of Chief State School Officers.

———. 2010b. *Appendix A: Research Supporting Key Elements of the Standards.* Washington, DC: National Governors Association Center for Best Practices and Council of Chief State School Officers.

Nist, S. L., and S. Olejnik. 1995. "The Role of Context and Dictionary Definitions on Varying Levels of Word Knowledge." *Reading Research Quarterly* 30: 172–93.

Ogle, D. 2007. *Coming Together as Readers*, 2d ed. New York: Corwin.

———. 2011. *Partnering for Content Literacy: PRC2 in Action: Developing Academic Language for All Learners*. Boston: Pearson.

Ogle, D., and A. Correa. 2010. "Supporting English Language Learners and Struggling Readers with the Partner Reading and Content, Too Routine." *Reading Teacher* 63 (7): 532–42.

Pany, D., J. R. Jenkins, and J. Schreck. 1982. "Vocabulary Instruction: Effects on Word Knowledge and Reading Comprehension." Learning Disabilities Quarterly 5: 202–15.

Pigada, M., and N. Schmitt. 2006. "Vocabulary Acquisition from Extensive Reading: A Case Study." *Reading in a Foreign Language* 18 (1): 1–28.

Pittelman, S. D., J. E. Heimlich, R. L. Berglund, and M. P. French. 1991. *Semantic Feature Analysis: Classroom Applications*. Newark, DE: International Reading Association (IRA).

Reed, D. K. 2008. "A Synthesis of Morphology Interventions and Effects on Reading Outcomes for Students I Grades K–12." *Learning Disabilities Research & Practice* 23 (1): 36–49.

Roop, P., C. Roop, and P. E. Hanson. 1987. *Keep the Light Burning, Abbie*. Minneapolis: Carolrhoda Books.

Roth, F., D. Speece, D. Cooper, and S. De la Paz. 1996. "Unresolved Mysteries: How Do Metalinguistic and Narrative Skills Connect with Early Reading?" *Journal of Special Education* 30: 257–77.

Ruddell, M. R., and B. A. Shearer. 2002. "'Extraordinary,' 'Tremendous,' 'Exhilarating,' 'Magnificent': Middle School At-Risk Students Become Avid Word Learners with the Vocabulary Self-Collection Strategy (VSS)." *Journal of Adolescent and Adult Literacy* 45: 352–63.

Schwartz, R., and T. Raphael. 1985. "Concept of Definition: A Key to Improving Students' Vocabulary." *Reading Teacher* 30: 198–205.

Scott, J., S. Flinspach, T. Miller, O. Gage-Serio, and J. Vevea. 2009. "An Analysis of Reclassified English Learners, English Learners and Native English Fourth Graders on Assessments of Receptive and Productive Vocabulary." In *58th Yearbook of the National Reading Conference*, ed. Y. Kim, V. Risko, D. Compton, D. Dickinson, M. Hundley, R. Jimenez, K. Leander, and D. Rowe, 312–29. Oak Creek, WI: National Reading Conference.

Scott, J. A., S. L. Finsplach, and J. L. Vevea. 2011. "Identifying and Teaching Vocabulary in Fourth- and Fifth-Grade Math and Science." Paper presented at the Literacy Research Association National Conference, Jacksonville, FL.

Scott, J. A., M. Hoover, S. L. Flinspach, and J. L. Vevea. 2008. "A Multiple-Level Vocabulary Assessment Tool: Measuring Word Knowledge Based on Grade-Level Materials." In *57th Yearbook of the National Reading Conference*, ed. Y. Kim, V. Risko, D. Compton, D. Dickinson, M. Hundley, R. Jimenez, K. Leander, and D. Rowe, 325–40. Oak Creek, WI: National Reading Conference.

Scott, J. A., T. F. Miller, and S. L. Flinspach. 2012. "Developing Word Consciousness: Lessons from Highly Diverse Fourth-Grade Classrooms." In *Vocabulary Instruction: Research to Practice*, 2d ed., ed. E. J. Kame'enui and J. F. Baumann. New York: Guilford.

Snow, C. E. 1991. *Unfulfilled Expectations: Home and School Influences on Literacy*. Cambridge, MA: Harvard University Press.

Snow, C. E., and Y.-S. Kim. 2006. "Large Problem Spaces: The Challenge of Vocabulary for English Language Learners." In *Vocabulary Acquisition and Its Implications for Reading Comprehension*, ed. R. K. Wagner, A. Muse, and K. Tannenbaum, 123–39. New York: Guilford.

Snow, C., J. Lawrence, and C. White. 2009. "Generating Knowledge of Academic Language Among Urban Middle School Students." *Journal of Research on Educational Effectiveness* 2 (4): 325–44.

Stahl, S. A., and M. M. Fairbanks. 1986. "The Effects of Vocabulary Instruction: A Model-Based Meta-Analysis." *Review of Educational Research* 56: 72–110.

Stahl, S. A., and B. A. Kapinus. 1991. "Possible Sentences: Predicting Word Meanings to Teach Content-Area Vocabulary." *The Reading Teacher* 45: 36–43.

Stahl, S. A., and W. E. Nagy. 2006. *Teaching Word Meanings*. Mahwah, NJ: Erlbaum.

Stahl, S., and S. Vancil. 1986. "Discussion Is What Makes Semantic Maps Work in Vocabulary Instruction." *The Reading Teacher* 40: 62–69.

Terman, L. M. 1916. *The Measurement of Intelligence*. Boston: Houghton Mifflin.

Tomeson, M., and C. Aarnoutse. 1998. "Effects of an Instructional Programme for Deriving Word Meanings." Educational Studies 24: 107–28.

Tunmer, W. E., M. L. Herriman, and A. R. Nesdale. 1988. "Metalinguistic Abilities and Beginning Reading." *Reading Research Quarterly* 23: 134–58.

van Kleeck, A., S. Stahl, and E. Bauer, eds. 2003. *On Reading Books to Children: Parents and Teachers*. Mahwah, NJ: Erlbaum.

Vosniadou, S., and A. Ortony. 1983. "The Emergence of the Literal–Metaphorical–Anomalous Distinction in Young Children." *Child Development* 54: 154–61.

Wagner, R. K., A. E. Muse, and K. R. Tannebaum. 2007. *Vocabulary Acquisition: Implications for Reading Comprehension*. New York: Guilford.

Watts-Taffe, S., C. L. Z. Blachowicz, and P. J. Fisher. 2009. "Vocabulary Instruction for Diverse Students." In *Handbook of Research on Literacy and Diversity*, ed. L. M. Morrow, R. Rueda, and D. Lapp. New York: Guilford.

Watts-Taffe, S., and C. G. Gwinn. 2007. *Integrating Literacy and Technology: Effective Practice for Grades K–6*. New York: Guilford.

Webster's New Collegiate Dictionary. 1979. Springfield, MA: G. & C. Merriam Company.

White, T. G., M. F. Graves, and W. H. Slater. 1990. "Growth of Reading Vocabulary in Diverse Elementary Schools: Decoding and Word Meaning." *Journal of Educational Psychology* 82: 281–90.

Willows, D. M., and E. B. Ryan. 1986. "The Development of Grammatical Sensitivity and Its Relationship to Early Reading Achievement." *Reading Research Quarterly* 21: 253–66.

Wright, T. S. 2012. "What Classroom Observations Reveal About Oral Vocabulary Instruction in Kindergarten." *Reading Research Quarterly* 47: 353–55. doi: 10.1002/RRQ.026.